P9-DMG-916

Being Dead Is No Excuse

Being Dead Is No Excuse

THE OFFICIAL SOUTHERN LADIES GUIDE
TO HOSTING THE PERFECT FUNERAL

Gayden Metcalfe
and Charlotte Hays

ISBN 1-4013-5934-5

FIRST EDITION

10

For a Trio of Belles

Anne Gayden Call
Julia Morgan Hall Hays
Josie Pattison Winn

CONTENTS

Being Dead Is No Excuse

1

Dying Tastefully in
the Mississippi Delta

After the solemnity of the church service and finality of the grave, the people of the Mississippi Delta are just dying to get to the house of the bereaved for the reception. This is one of the three times a Southerner gets out *all* the good china and silver: the other two are christenings and weddings. The silver has most likely been specially polished for the occasion. Polishing silver is the Southern lady's version of grief therapy.

Southern ladies have a thing about polishing silver. We'd be hard pressed to tell you how many of our friends and their mothers have greeted the sad news of a death in the family by going straight to the silver chest and starting to polish everything inside. Maybe it has something to do with an atavistic memory of defending our silver from the Yankees, but it does ensure that the silver will be sparkling for the reception, which almost always follows the funeral.

Friends and family begin arriving with covered dishes, finger foods, and sweets as soon as the word is out that somebody has died. We regard it as a civic duty to show up at the house and at the funeral because what we call a "big funeral" is respectful to the dead and flattering to the surviving relatives. After the cemetery, people go back to the house to be received by the family. Sometimes we talk bad about the deceased between the grave and the aspic, but we straighten up and are on best behavior the minute we get to the house.

During the reception, we gossip, tell stories about the deceased, and maybe indulge in a toddy or two. (Our county used to be "dry," but all that means is that we drink like fish, though we do make a special, if not always successful, effort to behave well at funerals—see "I Was So Embarrassed I Liketa Died," page 99.) You can't bury a self-respecting Deltan without certain foods. Chief among these is tomato aspic with homemade mayonnaise—without which you practically can't get a death certificate—closely followed by Aunt Hebe's Coconut Cake, and Virginia's Butterbeans. "You get the best food at funerals," we always say, and it's true. Funeral procedure is something that we all just know. A legion of friends working behind the scenes, coordinating the food, makes sure that the essential Delta death foods are represented in sufficient quantities. The best friend of the lady of the house, along with members of the appropriate church committee, swing into action without prompting. Almost everybody who attends the burial automatically stops by the house afterward, and it's a social occasion. One friend, on being thanked for attending a funeral, blurted out, "No, thank *you*! I wouldn't have missed it for the world."

The burial, which is solemn though rarely entirely devoid of humor, most likely takes place at the old cemetery on South Main Street. The old cemetery is one of the best addresses in Greenville, Mississippi. Being buried anywhere else is a fate worse than death in Greenville. The FFGs—that's First Families of Greenville—would simply refuse to die if they weren't assured of a spot. Not that the old cemetery is strictly FFG. Not by a long shot. Lola Belle Crittenden, bless her heart, had to plant a huge hedge around her ancestral plot. Why? The neighbors. "They're so tacky," Lola Belle huffed.

Although we always plan to have a good time at the reception, we revere the dead. Ancestor worship is as valid a form of religion as the Baptist, Methodist, Presbyterian, or Episcopal denominations in the Mississippi Delta. The cemetery is so sacred to the memory of our dead relatives that the whole town was up in arms when the local newspaper desecrated it. They did this by posing a high-school beauty queen in front of one of our most important graveyard monuments for a picture. Nothing has upset us quite so much before or since. For days on end nobody could talk about anything else, and the paper's Letters to the Editor page was filled with aggrieved missives. Old ladies shuddered at the thought that similar sacrileges might one day be committed on their graves. The paper had to grovel for forgiveness in print or face a serious drop in circulation. The newspaper was owned by Yankees, and, being outsiders, they just didn't know any better.

We're people with a strong sense of community, and being dead is no impediment to belonging to it. We won't forget you just because you've up and died. We may even like you better and visit you more often. As the former Presbyterian minister used to say in his justly celebrated funeral oration (I'd like to have a dime for every time I've heard it), dying just means you've "graduated."

We're good about remembering the dead with flowers on just about every holiday from Christmas Day to Groundhog Day. There's one family that was so intent on remembering Mama that they insisted on having her photographed in her coffin. The photographer balked but was finally persuaded. Afterward, the family flatly refused to pay. The eldest son explained why: "Mama looked so sad."

The old cemetery sees quite a bit of traffic, from the living and the dead. "This is a hard place to get out of," we invariably chortle when navigating our way through the gates and back onto Main Street. Some people, no doubt attracted by the prestige and the quiet, bucolic setting, have added to overcrowding problems by moving to the old cemetery years after they actually died. When Adelle Atkins, a widow, married James Gilliam, a Greenville widower, she insisted on bringing her late husband, Harry, along. She asked whether she could re-bury him on the Gilliam family plot.

Adelle's new in-laws—alas, already beginning to be packed

into their plot like sardines in a can—were appalled. They were obsessed with who would go where when the day came. And, besides, they hated the notion of new dead people coming in and just taking over. But Adelle is a determined woman, and she would not back down. Luckily for her, the Miss Finlays, two maiden lady schoolteachers, lived—or rather their dead relatives were buried—right next door to the Gilliams. Being old maids, they did not face the problem of potential overcrowding and were glad to have some extra cash. Adelle purchased half their plot and—*voila!*—Harry moved to Greenville.

We worry a lot about what will happen when the old cemetery fills up. Whenever Alice Hunt, who lives in New York, comes to Greenville, she goes straight to the cemetery and stretches out on her spot to reassure herself that nobody has encroached. She plans to wait for the final trumpet next to her Mama. Her big fear is ending up in the new part of the cemetery where, she says, she doesn't know a soul. There are a few fortunate families who don't have to worry about their future resting places because they still have private family cemeteries on plantations. This carries even more status than the old Greenville cemetery, but it's a lot of trouble. Jane Jeffreys Claiborne has spent her entire adult life fretting about the state of the old Claiborne cemetery on Woodville Plantation. Every time old Mrs. Claiborne got the sniffles, Jane Jeffreys lovingly put a gardener to work. She wanted the best for her mother-in-law, a funeral worthy of a Claiborne. Old Mrs. Claiborne would take one look, note the work going on in her honor, and immediately perk up. It worked better than penicillin. One day, of course, Mrs. Claiborne did die, and the cemetery looked so beautiful it made the rest of us envious. We were all thinking the same thing: I wish my family still had a private cemetery. Note the *still*. There are few things considered nicer than having your own cemetery.

Cremation is a possible solution to the overcrowding problem. But it's still a new and dicey proposition in the Delta. The last time somebody was cremated, his ashes were sprinkled from a crop duster. We all ran for cover. We liked him fine, but we didn't want him all over our good clothes. But you've got to say this: the folks who owned the property where the ashes were scattered had a darned good cotton crop the next year.

Maribell Wilson, whose father died in a hospital in Texas, had a different kind of problem. Maribell lived according to the cardinal rule of Southern ladyhood: Never learn to do anything you don't have to do. Maribell always needed somebody to drive her places. She finally relented and got a license and eventually became one of the worst drivers in the Delta, which is saying a lot. She was alone with her daddy when he died in Texas. Maribell had him cremated, as he had wished, and set out for home in a rental car with Daddy in a little box. Unfortunately, not being overly familiar with highway signs and such, Maribell got lost again and again and ended up on every back road between San Antonio and the Greenville city limits. It was hot as Hades, and Maribell kept the windows down. (She could have turned on the air conditioner, but nobody had ever showed her how.) When Maribell pulled into the driveway and opened the box, she was surprised to discover that Daddy had blown away on the ride home.

Then there was the man who took his Daddy to Memphis to scatter him in the big city where Daddy had grown up. He had to meet some friends for lunch and unwisely left Daddy in the office of a coworker, who carelessly put Daddy in her out-box. Unfortunately, somebody accidentally removed poor Daddy while she wasn't paying attention. Even though they searched high and low, Daddy was never found. Clearly, the cremation angle needs a little work to be viable in the Mississippi Delta.

Southern women always want to look their best—even if they happen to be dead. Our local undertaker, Bubba Boone, understands this. We brag that Bubba can make you look better than a plastic surgeon can, though, unfortunately, you do have to be dead to avail yourself of his ministrations. He did an outstanding job on Sue Dell Potter, a retired waitress. Sue Dell expressed a strange desire to go into the ground looking exactly as she had in her long-past waitress days. We went to call on Sue Dell at the funeral home and—lo and behold—she sported a big, teased bouffant and, unless you'd known her back when she was waiting tables and flirting up a storm at Jim's Café on Washington Avenue, you'd never have believed it was Sue Dell. But we feel certain Sue Dell was smiling down from heaven (with her now fire-engine-red lips) and thanking Bubba for his excellent work.

We'd better warn you not to put too much credence in the dates carved on the headstones. We Southern women tend to lie about our age—even when we're dead. Allison Parker, who always had a thing for younger men, made a complete fool of herself by knocking off five years. We died laughing when we saw the stone, because, if anybody looked her age, it was Allison Parker.

In the South, the casket is sometimes left open for visitation at the funeral home or when the body is brought home. There's nothing like a receiving line with somebody laid out a few feet away. Roberta Shaw used to be so afraid of dead bodies that she wouldn't allow even her own poor mother, Mrs. Robert Shaw, to fulfill her lifelong dream of lying in state on the dining room table in the big formal dining room at Runymeade Plantation.. She has since overcome this fear, and she wants to atone for what she believes must have been a huge disappointment for Mrs. Shaw. Now, whenever a friend or relative dies, Roberta crouches by the coffin and whispers to them. "Well, you'll never guess who just walked in," she whispered to Augusta Jones. Augusta, being dead, had absolutely no idea.

One of the rules in the South is that the newly dead are never left alone—somebody always sits with the coffin, day or night. Don't ask me why, but it wouldn't be right to leave a relative unattended. It used to be that most people took the body home before the burial and received guests with Mama right there. This custom, regrettably, isn't followed as often as it once was, though some families still uphold the tradition. The last time somebody did, it turned out sort of awkward. The body, which belonged to a local matriarch, stayed in the living room for an entire week. Somebody joked that the family was waiting for the out-of-town relatives to get the lowest airline fares possible. If you didn't make a sharp left turn into the dining room, you ended up face to face with the late wife of the town's leading lawyer.

We are sad at funerals, but there's no such thing as a funeral without a humorous moment. Once a visiting Episcopal minister took a step backward and fell smack into the grave. It certainly livened up the service. Since he went on to advocate advanced ideas, some of us wish we'd hit him on the head with a shovel. Not many have forgotten the time one of our more intellectual citizens died, and the Presbyterian minister, who'd known her forever, was out of town. The family rustled up a supply minister who'd never laid eyes on her. The night before the funeral, the family gathered to tell him all about the deceased, her fortitude in the face of a long sickness, her appreciation of art and literature. The sisters, knowing their big sister would want it, requested the minister to read some poetry, meaning maybe a bit of Shakespeare or Keats. But the visiting divine chose "Keep a-Goin'." (" 'Taint no use to sit and whine 'cause the fish ain't on your line; Bait your hook an' keep on tryin', keep a-goin'.") The bereaved sisters were doubled over with laughter. If you can't find something to laugh about, you will end up crying.

Here are some recipes that will come in handy if you want to die as tastefully as we do in the Mississippi Delta.

Bourbon Boiled Custard

While this boiled custard is delicious on its own, it also can be used to dress up a humdrum pound cake somebody has brought. We offer this recipe in memory of Josie Pattison Winn, of Greenville and New Orleans, who was known as the boiled-custard queen of the Mississippi Delta. Josie was famous for knocking on the front door with this luscious concoction practically before the body was cold. It was, well, to die for. Here's an easy version of our most comforting custard. The little touch of bourbon will help even the most distraught.

Ingredients:
1 cup sugar
4 eggs, beaten
2 tablespoons all-purpose flour
pinch salt
3 cups scalded milk
1 cup heavy (whipping) cream
2 teaspoons vanilla
¼ cup bourbon

In the top of a double boiler, combine the sugar, beaten eggs, flour, and salt. Then place the mixture over boiling water and slowly add the milk and cream. Stir constantly until the mixture coats the spoon. Immediately remove the mixture from the heat and add the vanilla and bourbon. Refrigerate. After this is well chilled, it will thicken. Enjoy this as is or serve it in a pitcher to put on a slice of cake or bowl of fruit. Multipurpose and prep time is not long.

Makes about six servings.

Aunt Hebe's Coconut Cake

We're already thinking about this coconut cake before the last "amen." This recipe comes from the late Hebe Smythe Crittenden, one of the renowned cooks of the Mississippi Delta. Gayden's mother excelled at making Aunt Hebe's Coconut Cake. Her mother (and we're sure Aunt Hebe) never used canned coconut. She can remember taking the ice pick and poking the eyes out of a coconut and draining the milk. Then, she'd get the hammer and crack the nut for someone to get the meat out and grate it.

Cake

Ingredients
1 cup unsalted butter
2 cups sugar
4 eggs, separated, at room temperature
2 ⅔ cups cake flour
2 teaspoons baking powder
½ cup fresh coconut milk
   (If you don't have time for real coconut milk,
   use 1 cup whole milk instead of ½ cup of each.)
½ cup whole milk
2 teaspoons vanilla

Before you start mixing, preheat the oven to 350°.

Cream the butter and sugar until fluffy. Beat in the egg yolks one at a time, incorporating well. Add the vanilla. Resift the cake flour with the baking powder and add sifted ingredients to the butter mixture.

Blend together one third of the milk mixture and one third of the butter mixture. Repeat until the mixtures are well incorporated. Beat the egg whites until stiff and fold them gently, by hand, into the batter.

You should have three 9-inch greased and floured pans. Divide the batter evenly among the pans and bake in a 350° oven for 25 to 30 minutes, or until the cakes are golden brown and they have pulled away from the edges of the pan. Cool for 5 minutes and then turn out.

When the cakes are completely cooled, you can ice them.

Real Icing

Ingredients

2 ½ cups sugar
½ cup water
2 ½ tablespoons clear Karo syrup
¼ teaspoon cream of tartar
2 egg whites
pinch of salt
2 ½ teaspoons vanilla
freshly grated coconut

Combine the sugar, water, and Karo and boil for about 5 minutes. Beat the egg whites with the cream of tartar until stiff. Pour the hot syrup into the beaten egg whites, slowly and beating all the time. Continue to beat this mixture until the icing is stiff and glossy. Add a pinch of salt and the vanilla. Spread a little icing between each layer. Then ice the sides and top, and garnish the whole cake with freshly grated coconut. You can use an electric hand mixer to beat this icing.

Serves twelve.

Tomato Aspic

Can you be buried without tomato aspic? Not in the Mississippi Delta, you can't. We've never been to a funeral where homemade aspic wasn't served. Store-bought aspic is available, but no self-respecting Southerner would be caught dead—sorry—eating it. If you've never had real tomato aspic, you're in for a treat.

This is the recipe Gayden uses most often because it is equally delicious with just mayonnaise, or with pickled shrimp, avocado slices, and other trimmings.

Ingredients

4 cups tomato juice
6 slices lemon
3 slices yellow onion, separated into rings
2 bay leaves
tops of one bunch of celery
several whole cloves
3 tablespoons horseradish
1 ½ teaspoons salt
1 tablespoon freshly ground black pepper
1 tablespoon lemon juice
1 tablespoon Worcestershire sauce (Lea & Perrins)
4 envelopes Knox unflavored gelatin
½ cup apple cider vinegar

Put the tomato juice, lemon slices, onion slices, bay leaves, celery tops, and cloves in a heavy pot and simmer for 20 minutes, more or less. While this simmers, mix together the gelatin and vinegar. Strain the tomato juice mixture and add the gelatin mixture. Stir until the gelatin has dissolved. No lumps! Add horseradish, salt, pepper, lemon juice, and Worcestershire sauce. Taste and correct seasoning.

Lightly oil a 6-cup mold. Pour the mixture into the mold and chill until firm, several hours or overnight. Overnight is best. Unmold on a bed of greens. If the aspic will not come out of the pan easily, run a knife around the edge or dip the pan into a sink of hot water—just for a second!

Serves ten.

I like to double this recipe.
In that case, I use a 10-cup bundt pan.

Homemade Mayonnaise

People act as if it takes an act of God to make homemade mayonnaise. It doesn't. But there is a real debate in Gayden's family as to whether homemade mayonnaise should be thick or thin. Her mother swears by runny, but Gayden's tends to be a little more firm. Of course, her mother makes hers by hand or with an old-fashioned Wesson oil-plunger contraption. This is now a collector's item, and Gayden uses a food processor. Here's her version:

Ingredients
   1 large egg
   1 ½ cups vegetable oil
   1 ½ tablespoons apple cider vinegar
   1 ½ teaspoons Tabasco sauce
   1 tablespoon lemon juice
   ½ teaspoon salt
   1 teaspoon white pepper

Assemble all ingredients. Put the egg in the food processor. Pulse for 30 seconds, and then add the oil slowly, while pulsing. When the desired consistency is reached, add the other ingredients until they are blended. This doesn't take very long! Of course, taste and adjust seasonings. But know: If you blend too long you will get a version that is too thick. Thin seems to be the preferred lady consistency.

Refrigerate for at least an hour, as the taste improves. We always have a jar of this in the icebox, and it hasn't killed us yet.

Makes about two cups.

Pickled Shrimp

Pickled shrimp are perfect with aspic. Without aspic, they are more appropriate for a cocktail party than for lunch after the funeral. Although our mothers wore dark colors and didn't go out socially for months after a death in the family, we no longer observe an official period of mourning, even in the Mississippi Delta. Still, we'd be shocked if you gave a cocktail party too soon. There's nothing to stop a friend from having a restorative cocktail party *for* you, however, as long as it's not done in unseemly haste.

Ingredients

5 pounds shrimp
7 teaspoons salt
1 cup celery tops
½ cup pickling spice
4 cups sliced onions
a few bay leaves
2 ½ cups salad oil
1 ½ cups white vinegar
5 teaspoons celery seeds
2 teapoons salt
1 jar (3 ¼-ounce) of capers

Drop the shrimp into boiling water to which salt, celery tops, and pickling spice have been added. Boil 8 minutes. Drain immediately and cool. DO NOT LET THE SHRIMP OVERCOOK. Peel and de-vein the shrimp. Using a large glass container, alternate layers of shrimp with onion slices and bay leaves.

Mix the salad oil, vinegar, celery seeds, and salt. Pour over the shrimp. Drain the capers and add them to the shrimp. Place the container in the refrigerator for at least three days. Turn once or twice a day, without fail.

To serve, drain, reserving liquid in case you have shrimp left over.

Serves twenty as an appetizer, twelve as a first course.

Mary Mac's Rolls

One of the most appreciated offerings is rolls. You can put them on the buffet table with the ham and homemade mayonnaise or hot mustard for sandwiches.

Ingredients
1 cup boiling water
$^3/_4$ cup shortening
1 $^1/_2$ teaspoons salt
$^3/_4$ cup sugar
2 eggs, beaten
2 packages active dry yeast
1 cup warm water
6 cups flour

Pour the boiling water over the shortening. Add the salt and sugar. Let the mixture cool, then add the eggs. Let the yeast stand in the warm water for 5 minutes. Then stir into the shortening/egg mixture.

Mix in the flour, a cup at a time. Transfer to a greased bowl in the refrigerator and let sit for at least two hours (The dough will keep in the icebox for several days). For the short term, a damp cloth cover will do, but longer term requires plastic wrap.

Roll the dough on a floured board. Cut the rolls out with donut cutter, brush with melted butter, and then fold them over. Place in a buttered pan and brush with more butter. About 15 to 18 rolls will fit in an 8-inch square pan.

Let rise 1 ½ hours in a warm place.

Bake at 375°, or until brown on top, about 10 to 12 minutes.

These rolls freeze beautifully. To do that, bake them until almost done, then freeze. Thaw and take to house of bereaved. Reheat before serving.

Makes about five dozen rolls.

Hot Mustard

Somebody always brings a supermarket platter of deli ham. We don't think we've ever been to a Delta funeral where there wasn't at least one. Fortunately, this supermarket fare can be transformed into something really good with homemade rolls, mayonnaise, and hot mustard (for more ideas, see "The Eternal Slick Ham Platter," p. 90).

Ingredients
- 1 cup dried mustard (Colman's preferred; big yellow can)
- 1 cup tarragon vinegar
- 1 cup sugar
- 3 eggs

Combine the mustard and vinegar, and soak overnight. Add the sugar. Beat the eggs and add them to the mixture. Cook in a double boiler over medium heat, stirring constantly until thick.

Keeps in the icebox for a long time . . . up to three months.

Makes about two cups.

Lace Cookies

Lace cookies are beautiful. They are not difficult. It just takes a bit longer because the dough spreads, so you get only a few per baking sheet.

Ingredients

    2 cups Quaker oats
    2 cups white sugar
    1 tablespoon flour
    $\frac{1}{2}$ teaspoon salt
    2 sticks unsalted butter
    2 eggs, lightly beaten
    1 teaspoon vanilla

Preheat oven to 350°. Combine the oats, sugar, flour, and salt. Melt the butter and pour it over the oats mixture while very hot. Stir until the sugar is completely melted. Fold in the eggs and vanilla, and mix until thoroughly blended.

Cover cookie sheets with aluminum foil. Drop scant teaspoons of dough at least 2 inches apart on sheets.

Bake about 10 minutes, or until the edges are lightly browned. These cook very fast: Watch carefully.

When the cookies have cooled, peel the foil off the backs and start another batch!

Remember, you need to have several sheets, or you will spend your entire afternoon in the kitchen. While you have one sheet in the oven baking, be sure you have another waiting to go in.

These freeze well if you use an airtight container.

Makes about five dozen cookies.

The Top Ten Funeral Foods

Tomato Aspic
  with Homemade Mayonnaise

Fried Chicken

Stuffed Eggs

Virginia's Butter Beans

Can't-die-without-it Caramel Cake

Homemade Rolls

Banana Nut Bread

Aunt Hebe's Coconut Cake

Methodist Party Potatoes

Tenderloin

2

The Methodist Ladies
vs. the Episcopal Ladies

Anyone in our neck of the woods who is not counting on immortality might want to give serious thought to taking the appropriate steps to become a communicant of St. James' Episcopal Church, before it is too late. No, belonging to St. James' won't necessarily get you into heaven. But it will ensure that you have a tasteful sendoff. Great vestments. No tacky hymns. St. James' sets liturgical standards for the Ark-La-Miss region (as the tristate area is known). St. James' is traditional and eschews novelty, though after members of the church vestry were impressed by the televised funeral of a female notable at the National Cathedral in Washington, D.C., a verger was added. Who could resist a verger? But other than that, St.

James' rarely changes so much as the position of a candlestick. Even the acolytes look the same from generation unto generation. That is because they are frequently the sons and nephews of previous acolytes. St. James' feels it has achieved liturgical perfection on earth. Ladies from the altar guild have been known to visit the Vatican only to sniff, "That's *not* how it's done at St. James'."

A nice funeral is good for everybody. If the family has been through a long, painful sickness, it's a chance to pull themselves together, spruce up, sober up, and put on their best dark clothes (white is acceptable during the Delta summer) and bid the dearly departed a formal farewell. We begin planning our funerals well in advance, not infrequently leaving behind detailed instructions. St. James' ability to offer parishioners the comforting knowledge that a dignified exit awaits them may be a central factor in maintaining its high membership rolls. Marguerite Blanton, who bragged that her family had been Episcopalians since the Crucifixion, once got so furious with the rector that she briefly entertained the notion of joining a band of renegade Episcopalians who held Sunday services in the community center. It was only the thought of her funeral being held at the community center that stopped Marguerite dead (so to speak) in her tracks. "You know," Marguerite said, "that's just not *me.*"

Southern Episcopalians wear their devoutness lightly. That's one reason they excel at funerals. They have a knack of comfortably mixing the formal and the casual, the proper and the relaxed (or perhaps the proper and the highly *im*proper).

Nowhere has this sensibility been better summed up than in the immortal words of Anne Dudley Hunt. (Of course, she was Anne Dudley Something-Else at the time.) One Easter Even—that's Episcopalian for the day before Easter—Anne Dudley was hobbling around the kitchen, bravely dyeing Easter Eggs, despite her knees, which were bruised black and blue. "I just don't know," Anne Dudley said. "Did I hurt my knees yesterday afternoon doing the Stations of the Cross? Or did I do it falling down drunk last night?" That, in a nutshell, is the spirit of Southern Episcopalianism. (To her credit, Anne Dudley remains a loyal daughter of St. James', even though the bishop put his foot down and flatly refused to let her have her fourth wedding there. The fifth time, she was too proud to ask.)

Greenville Episcopalians are sensitive enough to know that simply being dead doesn't mean you no longer care about social status. Nobody wants an ill-attended funeral. (If you look carefully, you'll notice older people moving their lips as they quietly count heads.) St. James' turns out in full force for its own. Penniless little old ladies and bank presidents alike get a nice turnout. For a *really* big funeral, dual membership—in St. James' *and* Alcoholics Anonymous—is the ticket. Episcopalians who have belonged to AA attract a standing-room-only crowd, without increasing the liquor bill for the reception. St. James' is so welcoming of mourners that, at a funeral, even if you accidentally sit in somebody else's pew, nobody gets really mad. (This doesn't hold true on other holidays, such as Christmas Eve, that attract the once-a-year worshipers; then regulars get their noses out of joint if they find a stranger in their pew.) A big St. James' funeral is well worth a lifetime of polishing altar brass and needle-pointing kneelers. (You don't have to go to church every Sunday, but the minister's honorarium should be handsomer for the parishioner who's darkening the door for the first time in years in a coffin.)

Yet another not-to-be-sneezed-at benefit: You won't be at risk for the nudge-producing eulogy. When Sally Bashford's dreadful old stepmother died, the Methodist minister lavishly eulogized her. You'd have thought somebody in town actually liked the old bat. There is rarely a eulogy at St. James', though in recent years a homily has been added to the funeral service. A brief note in the program explains that there won't be a eulogy. God doesn't "need to be reminded" about the deceased. Neither do the rest of us. While eulogists are going on and on about what a model citizen and devoted husband Mr. So-and-So was we're trying to keep straight faces. He was a notorious fanny pincher and crook, who was lucky not to have ended up behind bars. Yes, dead or alive, we'd all like to have praise heaped upon us. But isn't it safer, really, to wait until everybody is at home with a toddy? That way, if you can't stop laughing, you can claim you had too much to drink.

Speaking of the printed program, there are two schools of thought: Some believe that it should helpfully let outsiders know when to kneel and sit, without quite letting on that anybody thinks they don't know; old St. James' congregants— those in the eighty and above age bracket—are horrified that anybody would need to be *told*. Are there really people in the world who haven't bothered to learn what Episcopalians do? Should they not be punished? Fortunately, the sprightly Young Turks—sixty-five and under—are beginning to come into their own, and the program, with directions (an implicit acknowledgement that one actually knows people who do not belong to St. James'), is now thoroughly accepted. St. James' is, by the way, a middle-of-the-road church—embroidered chasubles and so on—but it's not a smells-and-bells kind of place. Of course, there were the late Miss Finlays, Little Miss Finlay and Big Miss Finlay, bless their hearts, two unmarried sisters—pillars of St. James'—who sat in the front row bobbing up and down like jumping jacks. They went in for crossing themselves and genuflecting. You could just about see what everybody was thinking: That's what comes of being a maiden lady who's never had sex.

You might think that by now all the St. James' selling points have been enumerated. They haven't. In addition to the dignified ambience and many other attractive features, St. James' is right across the street from the old Greenville cemetery. Talk about location, location, location. The walk over, after the church portion of the obsequies, is picturesque, especially in the fall, when you're not sweating bullets from the Delta heat. Nice English-county feel, which is popular in the Delta. The locale is also convenient for a reception, which is often held for family and friends in the parish hall. It follows the ceremony, and the "death committee" (more formally known as the Pastoral Care Committee) is in charge.

Attention to detail and borrowed silver are keys to its success. The committee rolls "big brown," the table, out into the parish hall, drapes it with a damask tablecloth, and puts a large silver coffee urn and tea service at one end and a large silver tray of goodies at the other. There is a chair for someone, usually an older lady, to pour. Once somebody put Coffee Mate on the table. The pourer quietly sent it back to the kitchen. A single overture to modern packaging: packets of low-calorie sweetener in a large silver wastebowl. Compotes on both sides of the table are filled with nuts. On the table are cheese straws; two cakes, each on a silver stand; and neat little squares of fudge cake (a famous local recipe; see Lowery's Fudge). A silver pitcher (borrowed, of course) sits on a special table for water drinkers. The table setups, if not the food, reflect an important article of the Episcopal credo: You can't be too thin or have too much silver. This is also just about the only time when two or three Delta Episcopalians are gathered together for any reason whatsoever and there's no booze. That's waiting at home.

Methodist Customs and Cuisine

Many local Episcopalians would be shocked to learn that St. James' is not the oldest church in the world. It is not even the oldest church in Greenville. That honor goes to the Methodists, who had a log-cabin church in the 1830s before St. James' was established in 1868. Also, the "Mother of Greenville," Harriet Blanton Theobold, was a devout Methodist. Mrs.

Theobold—many of whose descendants have naturally gravitated to St. James'—is accorded her matriarchal title because she donated land from her plantation to rebuild Greenville after it was burned down during the Wa-wuh. (Some people think Southerners refer to this unfortunate epoch as the War of Northern Aggression—that's not true; we just call it the Wawuh.) Mrs. Theobold is credited with introducing "Methodist cuisine" (in the parlance of an official Methodist history) to Greenville—which means she should also be honored as the "Mother of the Covered Dish Casserole."

Historically, Methodists are better behaved than Episcopalians. Lucy Mattie Trigg, who grew up as a Methodist preacher's daughter in Aberdeen, Mississippi (a town that, sad to say, is in the hill country and therefore not part of the more convivial Delta), remembered her Episcopal sister-in-law, who wasn't very devout, and who used to come and visit. This inlaw could shock everybody merely by going upstairs, turning on the Victrola, and dancing. She wasn't blood kin, so nobody could tell the infidel to stop. The family had to sit in stony silence in the parlor below as she desecrated the house.

From a social point of view, the Episcopalians and the Presbyterians, located a block away from each other, are competitive. Episcopalians who get mad at the rector zip over to the Presbyterian church until things cool down. When an elderly gentleman returned to St. James' after one such absence, parishioners noticed that he had pierced an ear. "That's what happens if you become a Presbyterian," everybody chortled, though there's absolutely no evidence that elderly Presbyterians are any more predestined to pierce their ears than elderly Episcopalians.

Though a number of old planter families still hew to the religion of the Wesley brothers, and there is certainly no spiritual or theological animosity, the culinary competition between the Episcopal ladies and the Methodist ladies is cutthroat. Episcopalians are snooty because they spurn cake mixes and canned goods, without which there would be no such thing as Methodist cuisine. Methodist ladies do great things with the contents of cans and boxes. If a survey were done of the winners of Pillsbury Bake-Offs, ten to one the majority would be Methodists. The casserole is the most characteristically Methodist foodstuff.

"You can always tell when a Methodist dies—there are lots of casseroles," said Lucy Mattie Trigg. A Methodist lady grocery-shops by wheeling her cart down the aisles and grabbing every can in sight. Her pantry looks like an arsenal, but she has on hand the makings of a fine casserole any time of the day or night. Because of this reliance on canned goods, the sodium content of Methodist funeral cuisine is high. If several Methodists die in a row, the ladies of the church complain that they can't get their wedding rings on; their fingers are too swollen. Methodist cooking, the mother lode of Greenville funerary fare, is delicious, but you must overcome snobbery and embrace canned soup, their favorite ingredient. The Methodist culinary genius might be summed up this way: Now you're cookin' with Campbell's. (See also "Comfort Foods: There Is a Balm in Campbells Soup," p. 141.) It should be noted that, when in a group, Episcopal ladies *say* they are purists and turn up their noses at Chicken Lasagna Florentine, a bubbly, cheesy concoction with everything from sour cream to buttered pecans, a Methodist favorite guaranteed to produce another funeral in short order. When polled anonymously, however, many Episcopalians admit to a secret preference for the eclectic Methodist goo. Fried chicken, though ecumenical, is yet another Methodist specialty, the dish traditionally served when the preacher comes to Sunday lunch.

The cookbooks put out by the Greenville Methodists abound in such treats as Hot Dog Stew, which the average St. James' cook would ostentatiously pass up—in public. While not entirely appropriate for a funeral, Hot Dog Stew, no doubt, helps Methodists weed out the (literally) faint of heart from their flock. Methodist cooking is definitely not for those who've recently had bypass surgery, unless they're angling to be the honoree at the next funeral.

A Methodist burial service is not quite in the same league with one at St. James'. There are robes rather than embroidered vestments and no rosy-cheeked acolytes. The Methodists are sort of the in-between church—not as formal as Episcopalians, yet not as rollicking as Baptists. "Methodists are frustrated Baptists who'd like to be Episcopalians," said Lucy Mattie Trigg. That is: They'd like to whoop and holler, but they are not deaf to the clarion call of upward mobility. When Methodists make the move to St. James', they must learn restraint. "They're never too peppy at the Episcopal church," sneered Lucy

Mattie, who visits occasionally with her son, now vying for a place on the vestry. At St. James', it would be truly amazing if you were put away to the tune of "Amazing Grace," a Methodist top ten. The elegiac "Oh, God, Our Help in Ages Past" is about as jolly as Episcopalians get. (For more on hymns, see "The Delta Funeral Hit Parade," p. 170.)

Methodist ministers often are former bad boys who smoked and drank and ran with the wild crowd before they saw the light and reformed. Episcopal clergy are nice boys (and now girls) who still like to smoke and drink and run with the wild crowd. But then, how can you reform when you've *always* had lovely manners? Episcopal rectors (please don't call them pastors!) tend to be preppy products of the Southern seminaries, in particular University of the South, fondly known as Sewanee, the Vatican for Southern Episcopalians. It is the be-all and end-all, located on a mountain in Tennessee, where some undergraduates, known as "gownsmen," wear academic robes around the campus all day. This helps feed the fantasy that they're really in Oxford, England, which Episcopalians like. Methodist preachers are less likely to dress in Brooks Brothers and clerical collar and more likely to be Bible thumpers. You'd never, for example, meet one with an alligator patch sewn on his clerical shirt, which one of our favorite Episcopal rectors sported in casual moments. These contrasting styles are important factors to keep in mind when planning your funeral.

Methodists are addicted to potluck events, a propensity manifesting itself in the funeral lunch at the church. There is a real sense of community, with all the ladies bringing their favorite casseroles or desserts. It's a nice way to take the burden off the family. But an ex-Methodist, now firmly ensconced at St. James', feels perhaps a bit too much of the burden is lifted. A few years at St. James' have attuned her to the finer things in mourning. "I arrived [at a Methodist funeral] with my horse-radish mousse on a cut-glass pedestal stand, and there were all these . . . Pyrex dishes," she sputtered. Everybody has to look down on somebody: For Methodists, there are Baptists. "The Baptists put little bitty marshmallows on their congealed salads," complained Methodist Lucy Mattie.

A final question: If you die a Methodist, will your friends and family enjoy the consolation of a nice, stiff cocktail? Delta Methodists are part Delta and part Methodist, which means they like a toddy now and then. Still, they aren't quite as imbued with—how shall we put it?—the cavalier spirit as Episcopalians. The Episcopalian ideal of a gentleman is a man who, if a lady falls down drunk, will pick her up off the floor and freshen up her drink. You practically have to be on the list for your second liver transplant before a Southern Episcopalian notices that you drink too much. They're not called Whiskypalians for nothing. One Christmas Eve at St. James', the Shaws found Bunny Parker passed out in their pew. Bunny had spent the hours leading up to the sacred rites at the Thunderbird Lounge on Main Street—famous the length and breadth of the Delta for having a *real* Thunderbird *inside*—and the miracle was that Bunny was able to find the church at all. Probably because he's very devout. The Shaws immediately forgave poor Bunny and, not wanting to interrupt his much-needed rest, stole somebody else's pew. It is a reasonably safe bet that being pie-eyed in church on Christmas Eve is not socially acceptable at any Methodist congregation in the Delta.

When a Methodist dies, you don't know if you're going to get bourbon or almond tea. If the family does break down and serve alcohol, they're likely to get a disapproving look when the minister comes to call. He will probably cast his disapproving gaze especially at the Episcopal minister, who, if paying a courtesy call, will fairly leap at the chance of a cocktail. When a Methodist minister drinks, it's for "purely medicinal purposes." If you feel your family will be so devastated by your departure that they'll require the solace of strong drink, join St. James'. Immediately.

The Ladies of St. James' Cheese Straws

Cheese straws have been served at every known occasion. Nothing compares with home-baked cheese straws. Cheese straws baked at home are to store-bought ones as fresh asparagus is to canned asparagus.

Delta cooks are incredibly protective of their recipes; nowhere is this more apparent than with cheese straws. One matron insisted we come to her house for a private lesson before she'd share her late mother-in-law's recipe.

Most cheese-straw recipes are pretty similar. The success depends on the cook's technique. Fortunately, proper technique is not that difficult; it rests on scrupulosity with regard to two basic rules: Always melt your butter before adding, and watch how you add the flour. Don't put it all in at once. Put it in slowly. Don't knead the dough, work it lightly with your hands—just enough to blend. Purists may omit the Worcestershire and Tabasco.

Ingredients

4 cups all-purpose flour, measure before sifting
2 scant teaspoons salt
1 ½ tablespoons cayenne pepper
approximately 4 sticks salted butter, melted
4 (10-ounce) packages of extra-sharp cheese,
    finely shredded

5 dashes Tabasco
5 dashes Worcestershire (Lea & Perrins)

Sift the flour, salt, and cayenne together. Work the melted butter into the shredded cheese (with your hands!). Note, the recipe reads 4 sticks of butter, approximately. Use the amount of melted butter to produce a consistency appropriate to your cookie press. Incorporate the flour mixture a little at a time (still using your hands). Add the Tabasco and Worcestershire to taste. Fill the tube of the cookie press. Using the ribbon disk produces a real bite, while the smaller disc produces the familiar squiggle.

Bake at 350° for approximately 12 minutes, or until firm to the touch and slightly brown around the edges. Squiggles take only about 10 minutes.

Makes about ten dozen.

Fried Walnuts

This recipe comes from the *Beyond Parsley Cookbook*, which was put out by the Junior League of Kansas City. Fried walnuts have become such a standard feature of the St. James' reception that few remember their origins do not lie deep in Delta culinary history.

Ingredients
    8 cups water
    4 cups English walnut halves
    ½ cup sugar
    cooking oil
    salt

NOTE: A pound of walnuts equals 4 cups.

Bring water to a boil, drop in the walnuts, and boil for one minute. Drain the nuts in a colander. Have water running very hot, or use a kettle of boiling water, and rinse.

Drain the nuts well again, immediately place them in a bowl, and coat with sugar.

Have the oil hot, and place the walnuts in the oil about one cup at a time, depending on the size of the pan. Fry until golden brown. Remove with a slotted spoon, drain, and place on wax paper in a single layer. Sprinkle with salt. Cool and store. These can be frozen in an airtight container. Left at room temperature, they remain tasty for a week.

Makes four cups of the three major food groups: salt, fat, and sugar

Lowery's Fudge Cake

No Greenville native of a certain age will ever forget the pleasure of biting into a piece of Lowery's fudge cake. It was sold exclusively at the old Lowery's Motel. We still remember how it was cut into squares and neatly wrapped in wax paper. After the Lowery ladies died and the motel restaurant became but a fond memory, custody of the fudge-cake recipe was passed to another lady of the church. It still arrives for the reception in perfect squares, wrapped in the traditional wax paper, though now the ladies of the Pastoral Care Committee unwrap it and arrange it on a silver tray. It never lasts long.

Ingredients
   2 sticks butter
   4 squares semisweet chocolate
   1 ¾ cups sugar
   4 eggs
   1 cup flour, sifted
   pinch of salt
   1 teaspoon vanilla
   1 cup chopped pecans

Preheat oven to 300°. Melt the butter and chocolate together. Add the sugar. Stir until melted. Cool slightly. With a wooden spoon, mix in the eggs, one at a time. Fold in flour and salt. Add vanilla and chopped pecans.

Some people like a lot of vanilla and a lot of nuts. I suggest 1 teaspoon vanilla and 1 cup chopped nuts. Sometimes more is better, Mies.

Pour the mixture into a buttered 9 x 11-inch pan. Bake for about 40 minutes. Start testing at 30 or 35 minutes. To be a purist, your straw for testing should come straight from the broom.

Florence Metcalfe's Variations:
Florence Metcalfe, Harley's mother and Gayden's mother-in-law, adapted the recipe and made it even lighter and more delicious. She separated the eggs and incorporated the yolks one at a time into the sugar. She then whipped the egg whites and folded them into the mixture. (The whites are beaten until they can hold a soft but not stiff peak.)

Makes eighteen squares

Million-dollar Pound Cake

This pound cake is served at St. James' receptions. As an offering to take to the house, it can't be beat. Not only is it a good dessert, but it also can be toasted in the morning for breakfast. Jane Hovas, a neighbor and one of the best Presbyterian cooks around, provided this recipe. Her original came from *Southern Living* magazine. It had been sent in by a friend of Jane's. We've tinkered with it over the years.

Ingredients
1 pound butter, softened
3 cups sugar
6 eggs
4 cups all-purpose flour
$\frac{3}{4}$ cup milk
1 teaspoon almond extract
1 teaspoon vanilla extract

Preheat the oven to 300°. Cream the butter; gradually add the sugar. Beat well. Add the eggs, one at a time, beating after each. Add the flour to the creamed mixture, alternating with milk. Begin and end with flour. Do not overmix. Add the flavorings.

Pour batter into a greased-and-floured tube pan (10-inch tube pan or 10-cup pan). Bake for 1 ½ hours, or until slightly firm to the touch. Cool in pan for ten minutes.

Serves twelve.

Mason-Dixon Curried Chicken Salad

You don't want the table to be monochromatic. There are about a thousand chicken salad recipes floating around the Delta. Not only is this one delicious, but because of the curry, it also adds a certain color to the table. Our curry powder south of the Mason-Dixon tends to be generic and weak, but it still adds a delightful zing. Three tablespoons of it is fine. However, 1 ½ of the *real* thing is quite sufficient. Remember, the taste amplifies as it chills.

Ingredients

4 to 5 pounds chicken breasts
   (dark meat is a no-no in chicken salad)
butter
¼ teaspoon salt
1 teaspoon pepper
2 ½ cups homemade mayonnaise
2 tablespoons soy sauce
½ lemon
1 ½ to 3 tablespoons curry powder
1 (10-ounce) package slivered almonds
2 cups sliced celery
2 (5-ounce) cans sliced water chestnuts,
   drained and rinsed
White seedless grapes, optional

Preheat oven to 350°.

Wipe the chicken breasts with butter, then sprinkle with salt and pepper. Wrap tightly in aluminum foil and place in a shallow pan. Bake for approximately 1 hour. Cool and cube the chicken. Mix the mayonnaise, soy sauce, lemon juice (a nice squeeze of fresh lemon), salt, and pepper. Start by adding 1½ tablespoons curry powder—gradually add more as you go.

Using a baking sheet, spread the almonds in a single layer, coat with butter, and toast until golden brown, about 15 minutes.

Add the mayonnaise mixture, water chestnuts, sliced grapes, and toasted almonds to cubed chicken. Correct seasoning and chill well.

Serves ten.

Virginia's Butter Beans

Although this recipe comes from the late Virginia Owens, a St. James' parishioner, Virginia's Butter Beans are made by everybody in town, and we can see why. The crumbled bacon is the crowning glory.

Ingredients
6 slices bacon, fried and crumbled
¼ to ¾ cup minced green onions
    (or yellow onions, if you please)
⅓ cup minced celery
⅓ cup bell pepper, minced
2 large cloves garlic, minced
2 tablespoons flour
2 cups drained canned tomatoes
Salt and pepper to taste
2 tablespoons brown sugar
2 (10-ounce) boxes frozen butter beans,
    cooked and drained

Preheat the oven to 350°.

Fry the bacon, remove from pan and crumble. In the same pan sauté the minced vegetables in the bacon grease. Add the flour, tomatoes, salt, pepper, and brown sugar. Add the cooked and drained butter beans. Adjust the seasonings, pour into a casserole, and top with crumbled bacon. Bake until bubbly.

Serves eight to ten.

This freezes well.

Ham Mousse

We know this must have been intended as a funeral dish: The original recipe called for unmolding the mousse and surrounding it with stuffed eggs—and, as everybody knows, stuffed eggs, like aspic, are a signature dish of death. We like to serve ham mousse with avocado mayonnaise.

Ingredients

- ³/₄ cup cold water
- 2 envelopes unflavored gelatin
- 1 ½ cups homemade mayonnaise
- 2 cups chopped ham
  (about a pound)
- ³/₄ cup chopped celery
- ½ cup chopped green pepper
- 2 ½ tablespoons grated onion
- ½ teaspoon white pepper
- 1 tablespoon fresh lemon juice
- ½ pint whipping cream,
  whipped

In a saucepan, add the unflavored gelatin to the cold water. Heat on low until the gelatin has dissolved. Gradually add this mixture to the mayonnaise, incorporating well. Chill in the refrigerator until slightly thickened. Add the ham, celery, green pepper, grated onion, white pepper, and lemon juice. Mix gently. Fold in the whipped cream. Pour into a quart mold and chill until firm.

Unmold on lettuce leaves and serve with avocado mayonnaise.

Serves ten.

Avocado Mayonnaise

After eating a generous helping of ham mousse and avocado mayonnaise, you're well on your way to an early demise! We're creating new customers as we go!

In the past, we didn't get always get good avocados in Greenville. Many years ago, Anne Gayden Call was so enthralled with the high quality of the fresh avocados in Florida that she sent her clothes back on the bus and filled her suitcases with the luscious avocados so that she could have the most delicious ones available.

Ingredients
homemade mayonnaise
(see recipe, p. 17)
2 avocados, diced
2 green onions, chopped
lemon juice

Start with the recipe for 2 cups regular mayonnaise. Before you turn your processor on, add the green onions and avocado. Process until the avocado is mixed into the mayonnaise. Add lemon juice to taste . . . maybe a tablespoon. Chill in an airtight container. If you are refrigerating the mayo for a while, add the avocado pit to the mayo to prevent it from turning brown . . . just remember to remove the lovely pit before serving!

The Methodist Ladies' Chicken Lasagna Florentine

For once, we're at a loss for words. Pecans and lasagna? But this is the quintessential Methodist death dish, and it's so good it'll kill you.

Ingredients

6 lasagna noodles, uncooked
1 (10-ounce) package chopped frozen
    spinach, thawed
2 cups cooked, chopped chicken
    (about 3 medium breasts)
2 cups shredded cheddar cheese
⅓ cup finely chopped onion
¼ to ½ teaspoon ground nutmeg
½ teaspoon salt
2 teaspoons white pepper
1 tablespoon soy sauce
1 can (10 ¾-ounces) cream of mushroom soup
1 (8-ounce) carton sour cream
⅓ cup homemade mayonnaise
¾ cup freshly grated Parmesan cheese
    (or to taste)
Butter Pecan Topping
    (see below)

Preheat oven to 350°.

Cook the noodles according to package directions, drain and set aside. Drain the spinach well, pressing between layers of paper towels. Combine the spinach, chicken, cheddar cheese, onion, nutmeg, salt, pepper, soy sauce, soup, sour cream, and mayonnaise in a large bowl; stir well to blend.

Arrange half the lasagna noodles in a lightly greased 11 x 7 x 1 ½-inch baking dish. Spread half the chicken mixture over the noodles. Repeat this procedure with the remaining chicken mixture and noodles. Sprinkle with Parmesan cheese and Butter Pecan Topping. Bake, covered, for 55 to 60 minutes, or until hot and bubbly. Let stand for 15 minutes before cutting.

Serves eight.

Butter Pecan Topping

Ingredients
    2 tablespoons butter or margarine
    1 cup chopped pecans

Melt the butter in a skillet over medium heat; add the pecans and cook for 3 minutes. Cool completely.

Poulet John Wesley

Everyone loves fried chicken—it's *the* ecumenical dish. One of the reasons it's so good for funerals is that it can sit on the sideboard for hours and still be delicious.

Ingredients
    1 chicken, cut up . . . a nice,
       medium-size yard bird
    2 eggs
    2 cups whole milk
    2 cups flour
    salt
    black pepper
    ½ teaspoon baking powder
    fat for frying (Crisco, vegetable oil,
       or a combination. Crisco is a nice
       way of saying "lard.")

Lightly beat the eggs and blend with the milk. Combine the flour, salt, pepper (a generous amount), and baking powder in a doubled brown grocery bag . . . shake to mix. Dip each piece of chicken in the egg/milk mixture. Shake chicken, one piece at a time, in the bag of flour until well coated (at this point, some cooks prefer the double-dip method where they repeat the egg-wash-and-flour procedure).

Using a preseasoned black-iron skillet, heat enough oil to almost cover the chicken. When you drop the chicken in, the fat sizzles! Frying is an art. The real art involves the grease, which must not burn but cook at an even, medium-hot level. Cooking time will vary according to the size of the piece of chicken. Approximately 20 minutes.

Serves three to four.

NOTE: Do not crowd the chicken when frying. Turn only once, when golden brown on one side. Remove pieces from the skillet and drain them on a brown grocery bag that has been covered with a layer of paper towels . . . soaks up extra grease better than anything!

Methodist Party Potatoes

Party Potatoes might sound a bit jolly for a funeral, but no self-respecting Delta Methodist is buried without them. Note to purists: If you refuse to cook with corn flakes, skip this recipe.

Ingredients
1 2-pound package hash browns
10 ounces grated sharp cheddar cheese
½ cup chopped onions
1 pint sour cream
1 can (10 ¾-ounces) cheddar cheese soup, not diluted
1 teaspoon salt
2 teaspoons pepper, coarsely ground

Topping
2 cups corn flakes
1 stick butter

Preheat oven to 350°.

Prepare the hash browns according to the package directions. Combine the cooked hash browns with the other ingredients and place in a buttered 13 x 9-inch casserole dish. Top the casserole with corn flakes and dot with butter. Bake 40 minutes, or until golden, crisp, and bubbly. After you've eaten your fill, ask your doctor to add Lipitor.

Serves eight.

Vegetable Casserole

You can tell a Methodist recipe because it almost always has a step that reads, "Blend sour cream and cheese." This is standard at the church lunch. While it might sound awful to the uninitiated, it's the apotheosis of food to die for.

Ingredients

1 can (14 ½-ounces) French-cut
   green beans
1 can (15 ¼-ounces) shoe-peg corn
1 can (8-ounces) sliced water chestnuts
salt
black pepper
1 can (10 ¾-ounces) cream of celery soup
½ cup sour cream
½ cup minced onion
½ cup grated sharp cheddar cheese
1 stick Oleo
1 roll (35) Ritz crackers
½ cup slivered almonds

Preheat oven to 350°.

Drain the beans, corn, and water chestnuts. Mix in a greased 9 x 13-inch pan (2 quarts). Add salt and lots of black pepper. Mix the soup, sour cream, onions, and cheese. Spread over bean and corn mixture.

Melt the Oleo and mix with crushed Ritz crackers. Spread over the top of the above mixture. Sprinkle the almonds on top. Bake for 45 minutes.

Serves eight.

NOTE: We use whole-wheat crackers—37 to a roll—and no-fat sour cream.

Martha Jane Howell's Pineapple Casserole

Yes, you read that right: pineapple casserole. This is a wonderful and easy-to-make dish that goes especially well with baked ham or a green-bean casserole.

Ingredients
   2 cans (20-ounces) crushed
      pineapple
   5 tablespoons flour
   $\frac{1}{2}$ cup sugar
   1 cup (8-ounces) grated sharp cheese
   Ritz crackers
   1 stick butter
      (real butter—no substitutes)

Drain the pineapple. Grease a 2-quart oblong casserole dish and put the pineapple in the bottom. Sift the flour and sugar together, blend it with the cheese, and then sprinkle on top of the pineapple. Cover with crushed Ritz crackers (a tube or a tube and a half will do nicely). Melt the butter and pour over the top. Bake at 350° for about 30 minutes.

Serves eight.

Mint and Almond Teas

Think of these teas as Methodist chardonnay. Methodists rarely drown their grief in anything stronger than flavored tea. Mint tea and almond tea are refreshing in the Delta summer and won't cause you to say things you regret later. The mint tea is a legacy of a long-gone local minister. (No doubt some rector of St. James' has passed down his favorite highball recipe.)

Almond tea ingredients
    4 cups strongly brewed tea
    ¾ cup water
    1 can (60-ounce) frozen lemonade,
        thawed
    1 cup sugar
    2 teaspoons almond extract
        (a little goes a long way)

Combine all ingredients. Stir it until the sugar is dissolved, and serve over ice.

Makes about twelve cups

Mint Tea

16 cups water (one gallon)
7 tea bags
7 sprigs fresh mint
rind of 3 lemons
juice of 7 lemons
2 cups sugar

Bring half the water to a boil. Add the tea bags, mint, and lemon rinds; steep for 12 minutes. Add the lemon juice and sugar to the remaining 8 cups of water. Mix with the tea and serve over ice. For funeral purposes, I wouldn't garnish each glass with mint, though that's a nice touch for less-somber occasions. Serve it from a glass pitcher.

Makes about two gallons.

The Eternal Pantry—
A Legacy for Your Children

Like those who wait for Elijah, the Delta cook is always prepared for a funeral. She does this in two ways: First, there is always a summer funeral frock and a winter funeral frock hanging cleaned in her closet, ready to be donned at a moment's notice. Second, she always has a well stocked pantry that allows her to throw together a delicious casserole or sweet by the time Bubba Boone has finished putting the lipstick on the corpse.

The items in the death-ready pantry comprise mostly nonperishables that will outlive us all. Consider the Eternal Pantry a legacy to leave to your children . . . along with a copy of this book!

Duncan Hines yellow cake mix
Tomato juice
Knox unflavored gelatin
Rotel tomatoes
Evaporated milk
Condensed milk
Canned shrimp
Durkee Famous Sauce

Worcestershire sauce (Lea & Perrins)

Tabasco sauce

Canned artichoke hearts

Water chestnuts, sliced

Pimientos (in jars)

Slivered almonds

Cream of mushroom soup, if you must

Green beans, whole Blue Lake variety

French's canned french-fried onions

Ritz crackers, whole-wheat variety

Chicken stock (Of course, in an ideal world, you
would make it yourself, but this is not an ideal
world.)

Kraft mayonnaise (A sacrilege? Yes, but nevertheless
advisable.)

Hellmann's mayonnaise (too sweet now to be the
all-purpose store-bought mayo)

A well-stocked bar and wine closet (Somebody
is always going to use it, and it'll never spoil—
a good investment.)

*NOTE: If you combine any three items
of like value on this list, you're likely
to have made a funeral casserole.*

3

Who Died? Stuffed Eggs, Etiquette, and Delta Pâté

People in the Delta look better dead, whether in their coffins or obituaries. Although we sometimes succumb to the temptation to speak ill of the dead—usually in the car on the way from the cemetery to the house—we don't believe you have to have won a Nobel Prize to get a good obituary. A glowing obituary is practically a birthright in the Delta, and it should be a write-up that would not only please the deceased but gratify those left behind. Usually it does. Whatever you think about the purpose of the funeral, the obituary *is* for the living—at least, in the Delta, it is. Here's how it always worked in the past: A member of the bereaved family just did the write-up, handed it in to somebody at the paper they'd known their whole lives, and it ran, pretty much as written, as a news story. Think of it this way: While Bubba Boone prettifies the mortal remains for the visitation, somebody else touches up the incorporeal remains for the newspaper.

We all want to be accorded our due respect, dead or alive. Mrs. Robert Shaw refused to fly on an airplane with the local newspaper editor. He had won a Pulitzer Prize, and Mrs. Shaw reasoned that in the event of a crash killing all aboard, the editor's death would overshadow hers. He was so famous that he'd get the top billing, and Mrs. Shaw would not be allowed to shine at this pivotal moment in her life. "I would absolutely hate to be listed as an 'also on the plane,'" Mrs. Shaw said. If she went out to the airport to fly to Memphis for a day of shopping and the editor was getting on the plane, Mrs. Shaw turned right around and went home. By waiting a day, she could rest assured that, in the event of a crash, she would get all the attention she deserved.

When it comes to the obituary, it is important not to lie outright. In the same way that you don't want Bubba Boone to make you look like a wax doll when your time comes, you do not want to make deceased relatives unrecognizable in their own obituaries. There's a difference between touching up a few details and an extreme make-over. In an obituary, you must strive to make the deceased look their best—but not to look like somebody else. After all, this is a moment for which they've been waiting all their lives. Selectivity is the key to success in this delicate undertaking.

In the Delta, we are blessed to have before us fine examples of the art of helping the dead put their best foot forward without actually lying. We have been doing this for a long time. In 1905, Joshua Ridgeway was shot and killed in a barroom brawl in front of the old Hotel Greenville. For his tombstone, the family selected "Blessed are the peacemakers." It was an inspired choice. While it doesn't actually deny that Mr. Ridgeway died in a vicious gunfight, in which he killed two other gentlemen, it does imply that he just happened to be in the wrong place at the wrong time and might even have been engaged, unsuccessfully, in trying to talk the others into laying down their arms. Of course, they would have known better than to fall for that.

A well-known local roué and cad, Harvey Magruder, was shot and killed for seducing another man's wife. His children simply bought the biggest stained-glass window available and put it in the First Methodist Church in loving memory of Harvey and Mrs. Harvey. Some wit suggested that the scene should have depicted Mary Magdalene instead of a virgin martyr. Still, there are few things more respectable than your own stained-glass window.

When our beloved Augusta Jones died, there wasn't a dry eye for miles around. She had battled valiantly with a long illness, and we loved her dearly. But even her staunchest supporters recognized that some of Augusta's life choices made for an obituary writer's worst nightmare. She had graduated an art history major from Agnes Scott College in Atlanta, Georgia—so far so good—and then high-tailed it to New Orleans' French Quarter. This is where, from the standpoint of her eventual obituary, things careened off course. Augusta embraced the hippie way of life. She had so many hippies staying in her apartment at one point that it looked like a hippie commune, if hippie communes had antique four-poster beds. The only time her apartment was hippie-free was when she sent them to Florida for an all-expense-paid vacation. Whenever anybody went to New Orleans and saw Augusta—whose ancestors *could* have come over on the *Mayflower* if they hadn't belonged to the Established Church—in her tie-dyes selling flowers from her cart in Jackson Square, it was all they could talk about for weeks on end. Augusta also made quite a name for herself singing the blues in nightclubs on Bourbon Street. She had a beautiful voice, and we thought of her as the Janis Joplin of the old plantation set. You are beginning to see the problem. But this is where the skill and tact native to us Southerners came into play. It was a beautiful obituary that chose to focus on Augusta's charitable endeavors. Like all good pieces of writing, it was informative. Some of us had not realized that Augusta belonged to the Junior Auxiliary.

Southern ladies are notoriously vague, and so, too, must their obituaries be, if their families are to be pleased. "This is Mama's first night as a college girl," Sally Morgan Gilliam, Miss Olivia Morgan Gilliam's daughter, observed after perusing her mother's obituary. The whole family shushed her. But you did have to read the write-up very, very carefully to ascertain that Olivia Morgan had in fact dropped out of All Saints in the eleventh grade. As opposed to, say, being valedictorian and going on to the junior college, which casual readers might have been forgiven for thinking. At the time her formal education ended, Miss Olivia had stated: "I can't go to parties and date boys and take all these hard courses. I have to make a choice." But why worry when you can go to college posthumously? If the theme of the eulogy is, "You've graduated," the theme of the obituary is, "You're promoted." Didn't win the 4-H Club award for the county's fattest pigs in life? You can win it in death, with the right obituary writer.

And this was before the advent of the paid obituary, which has thrown us into a quandary—you can lay it on even thicker, of course, but some of us find it beneath our dignity to pay to get our names in the paper. Most families do ultimately realize that it would be a shame not to see their dead remembered in the paper. Note: That's dead, because being dead is socially acceptable, while being called somebody's dead "loved one" is tacky. (We will speak later about how to talk about death, and how not to, in the Delta.) In Mississippi, the decedent's forbears unto—oh, about three or four generations, may rate a mention. If the decedents' stellar achievements include membership in the Order of the First Families of Mississippi (note to Yankees: This is a real organization), this affiliation will be prominently noted. The florid style of the past—"A Delta planter has been called to his rest . . ." has been considerably toned down, but quite understandably, some kindhearted obituary writers are unable to resist the temptation to bestow in death some honor withheld in life. It is never too late to be Rotary Man of the Year, as long as the year is so long ago that nobody remembers.

In Southern towns, there always used to be somebody at the newspaper whose job it was to arrange the wedding notices and obituaries in the proper order. This was most often an intellectual spinster from an old but impoverished family. She knew not only who everybody's parents were but who their grandparents were. She ruled the society page with an iron hand and cared intensely whether or not someone was top drawer, even if that was the funeral house's cooling drawer, where they happened to be reposing while awaiting the services of the cosmetologist. The obituaries are now arranged in alphabetical order. This may be because so many local papers are now owned by Yankees who don't know what's what or who's who. Or it may be due to a shortage of spinsters willing to devote their every waking moment to making sure that, dead or alive, people know their place. This new system can be jolting for old timers. If Mrs. Minor Millsaps had had the good fortune to die ten years earlier, she would have automatically led off the obituary column for her day. When she actually did die, she had the misfortune to shake the mortal coil on the same day as Hound Dog Hurley. In our decadent modern world, H comes before M, even if Hound Dog's main claim to fame was having taken twelve years to graduate from Ole Miss. (No mean feat.) Subsequently, he spent much of his adult life sitting on his front porch watching the traffic go by. A lot of the old ladies thought it was nervy that Hound Dog had the audacity to die when he did. It just confirmed what they'd thought about him all along: Nervy.

You don't need a high-school diploma to know that there are nice and not-nice ways to talk about death. "If *e-vuh* anybody says somebody has passed away," Olivia Morgan sternly admonished her girls, "look perplexed, roll your eyes, and say, 'Was she playin' bridge?'" Nice people do not pass away. They die. Our ancestors have been dying for hundreds of years, and we plan to continue this tradition. It is an integral part of the Southern way of life. It is also one of the rare instances when we refuse to sugar coat.

Still, the Delta note-writer expresses herself delicately. You never say you're writing because Uncle Willie keeled over dead when getting up for his third helping of fried chicken at the Rotary Club buffet; you are writing because Uncle Willie has been "lost." A well-wrought note of condolence would convey to the uninformed the impression that Uncle Willie has once again escaped his nurse and is still wandering around the Greenville mall with Alzheimer's.

Mrs. Gilbertson of Leland came from a fine family that has been dying in the Delta for many generations—though none quite like Mrs. Gilbertson. She was hacked to death with the garden shears. Her daughter did the hacking. Everybody always said that old Mrs. Gilbertson was difficult, and one day Anna Sue just got fed up. It made all the papers, even out of state. "We were just lucky to have her for as long as we did," Mrs. Gilberston's sister Maude observed meekly, as we put the stuffed eggs on the sideboard. Miss Maude paused and added, "Of course, she might not have wanted to go the way she did." No, she might not have. Still, she was probably looking down from heaven, pleased that, aside from Anna Sue, everybody in her family was behaving, and speaking, in such a proper fashion. "Going," you see, is another acceptable way of indicating that someone has departed for that bourn from which no man returns. The Gilbertson departure really hit us hard. "The *real* tragedy of the Gilbertson murder," observed one Delta matron, "was that Anna Sue's youngest daughter didn't get to make her debut." Still, things could have been a lot worse. While Anna Sue was serving her time in the Parchman State Penitentiary, everybody said she was the most popular prisoner there. She taught other prisoners to read. She did this by pretending she was still in the Junior Auxiliary (the small-town version of the Junior League) and they were her projects. Her old friends didn't drop her, either. While she was in Parchman, she received a home-cooked meal every Sunday, with real silver and a cloth napkin, courtesy of her loyal bridge club. After all, Anna Sue may have hacked her mother into tiny pieces, but she was still a lady. It was her ladylike behavior, along with her husband's connections, that contributed to her early release. She was welcomed back to Leland, where she taught Sunday school at the Baptist Church. Some worrywarts always said, "Anna Sue will kill again." But she never did. As far as we know.

Like a bubbling corn-flake casserole, or a tray piled high with dainty pimiento sandwiches with the crusts cut off, a proper sympathy note soothes. Notes are almost as important as food, and Southern mothers work hard to ensure that their children grow up able to write a good one. They know they will be judged on this. "Whenever somebody writes me a blah note, I say, 'I bet her mother wasn't a Southern girl,'" said Sally Morgan Gilliam. Nobody wants to be talked about in that fashion. A note from a Southern girl never has a fill-in-the-blank feel. There is nothing generic about it. A Southern girl has to stop herself from gushing more than Old Faithful. If she is writing a thank-you note for a toaster, she doesn't just say thank you. She tells you about every little ol' thing she's ever toasted in it or is likely to toast in it. In a sympathy note, she doesn't say that Uncle Willie who has been lost will now be missed—she recalls the cute bow ties Uncle Willie always wore. She does not recall that he also had a cute mistress named Lorene.

After Taylor Tuthill lost her favorite third cousin once removed, she came home from Memphis for the funeral. Her thank-you note to the family who put her up for the sad occasion was a model. Her note was superb in its observation of the two main rules of note writing, as interpreted by the Southern girl. They are: 1) Lay it on with a trowel; 2) Include an anecdote that makes the note personal. This lets the recipient know that this isn't just any old note—it's for them alone. (You don't need a different personal anecdote for every note. The Southern girl fully expects to recycle the PA.) "I want to thank you one more time for being there for me. You are the kindest people in the world, if not the universe, and I am absolutely certain that nobody would be sweeter about my letting Buckwheat out of his pen. I pray that he will show up to take his place in the duck blinds with George, who is the greatest duck hunter in the world," Taylor Tuthill began. "Speaking of dogs," she went on, setting the stage for a brilliant execution of Rule Two, "I couldn't believe it when my brother Edmund showed up with his new girlfriend, and she brings this two-pound, long-haired dog named Peaches." What could be a better PA than, "When Peaches started barking in church, I thought, 'God help us now.' Again, I cannot thank you enough." Nobody could accuse Taylor's mother of not being a Southern girl.

One of our dearest old ladies used to give all correspondence that came to her "the finger test" and bemoan those that did not pass. The finger test is when you run your index finger along the monogram to see if it's really engraved. Naturally, we consider this shallow—or we have tried to convince ourselves that we consider this shallow. We have not always succeeded. Of course, we invented shabby genteel down here, and we really don't mind if a family scrimps because of actual economic hardship. We are not pleased, however, when somebody who made a good crop last year resorts to that cheesy, pre-printed stationery supplied by the funeral home. A death is the time for the best stationery you can afford.

Although Miss Edith Wharton was a Yankee lady, a passage in one of her books has special resonance for the Southern lady. There is a scene in *The Custom of the Country* when Undine Spragg's mother is trying to reply to an invitation from a social arbiter and wavers before signing her name.

She gets it right the first try—just plain Leota Spragg. Then, trying to sound proper, Leota B. Spragg goes on to substitute the most incorrect signature possible: Mrs. Leota B. Spragg. Maddening. Maddening. Maddening. For a Southern reader, this passage is almost painful. Like Miss Wharton, we are obsessed with matters of form, possibly because we've experienced hard times when good manners were all we had left. The Delta is the last place in the world that still uses the old-fashioned form of addressing a divorced lady as Mrs. Maiden Name + Ex-Husband's Name. "I am no longer Mrs. Culloden Smith, and there is no such person as *Mrs.* Jane Smith, though *I* am Jane Smith," Jane Smith explained to her daughters, adding, "My formal title is Mrs. Jones Smith." That's because her name was Jane Jones before she married that good-for-nothing Culloden Smith IV. Of course, a lady never signs a personal note *Mrs.* Anybody. This is noblesse oblige— you pretend you think the recipient is your equal. No matter who the recipient, you sign your given (first) name. In this, the Southern lady follows the lead of Queen Elizabeth, who signs herself *Elizabeth R.*

As we've noted, the obituary may not tell you exactly who has died, at least not so you'd recognize them. And there is one food in the Delta that, if it doesn't tell you who died, it tells you somebody has died. Stuffed eggs are associated so closely with death that any time you see the lady of the house getting down the egg plate, you might well ask, "Who died?"

Most Delta families possess a china egg plate with oval

indentations for stuffed eggs. For some reason, it rarely leaves its shelf unless there has been a death. "Whenever somebody dies in the Delta," said Eleanor Vicks, "you just automatically take stuffed eggs and a bottle of wine. Unless you're Methodist, and then you just take the eggs." Pimiento cheese isn't just for death. We eat so much of it that it's sometimes called Delta pâté. Like stuffed eggs, pimiento cheese, in all its glorious guises, is a funeral staple. When we think of aspic, dainty pimiento cheese sandwiches on whole-wheat bread with the crusts cut off, and stuffed eggs, we almost look forward to funerals. Just kidding.

Stuffed Eggs

A "polite civil war" rages over whether sweet or savory is preferable in stuffed eggs. Savory egg partisans tend to regard the palates of the sweet-egg camp as less sophisticated. We must need a culinary course, because we are fond of both. One of the attractions of stuffed eggs, whichever camp one belongs to, is simplicity: Peel hard-boiled eggs and cut in half lengthwise. Remove yolks and mash. Add to yolks the mixture made from listed ingredients. Stuff the eggs and garnish, then chill the stuffed eggs, not because they'll kill you if you don't, but because putting them in the icebox for a bit gives the flavors an opportunity to mingle. Some garnishing suggestions: sliced black olives or stuffed green olives, crumbled crisp bacon, minced parsley, or the traditional sprinkle of paprika.

Some ingredients not common to the usual egg combinations are minced shrimp, horseradish, diced pimientos, capers, or any combination thereof. Oh, and by the by, we prefer to call them stuffed eggs instead of deviled eggs. The reason is lost in the mists of history.

Anchovy Stuffed Eggs

For advocates of the savory school of stuffed eggs, it doesn't get much better than this recipe.

Ingredients
    6 hard-boiled eggs
    4 anchovies, well drained
    3 teaspoons lemon juice
    3 tablespoons homemade mayonnaise
    fresh pepper
    2 tablespoons freshly chopped parsley
    1 small jar (2 ounces) pimientos, well drained
    1 small bottle (3 ¼ ounces) capers, well drained

Crisscross the pimientos over the top of the egg and dot the crisscrosses with the capers.

Makes one dozen servings.

Sweet Stuffed Eggs

You'll need a big egg plate for this recipe—it makes twenty-four servings. By the way, it's tasty but not fancy—notice we use plain old French's mustard instead of some rarefied moutarde. These are what we call peckerwood eggs.

Ingredients

1 dozen hard-boiled eggs
sweet pickles or sweet pickle relish
    (start at 2 teaspoons and continue to taste)
1 tablespoon mayonnaise
2 teaspoons French's (!) yellow mustard
1 teaspoon onion, finely minced
2 tablespoons Durkee Famous Sauce
salt and pepper to taste
paprika for garnish

Makes two dozen servings.

Todd Lane's Eggs

Like the corn-flake casserole, this recipe sounds bad but tastes good. If you make it once, the jar of Kraft sandwich spread will be in your pantry when you die—this is the only recipe we know that calls for it.

Ingredients
　　6 large eggs
　　2 tablespoons finely minced celery
　　1 ½ tablespoon Kraft sandwich spread
　　1 teaspoon Worcestershire sauce (Lea & Perrins)
　　¼ teaspoon Tabasco
　　½ teaspoon salt
　　chopped parsley, no more than a quarter cup
　　paprika to be sprinkled as garnish

Makes one dozen servings

Southern Pâté: Pimiento Cheese

A writer once called our area "the most Southern place on earth." Pimiento cheese might just be called the most Southern dish on earth. Pimiento cheese has been dubbed "the paste that holds the South together." We'd pick Southern *pâté* over foie gras any day of the week. As with stuffed eggs, a sweet vs. savory war continues, with no signs of a truce. Cooks who belong to the latter camp look down their noses at those who put in a dab of sugar—and vice versa. The flavor is actually derived from the binding agents. That's why those who say it's the homemade mayonnaise that makes us love pimiento cheese have a point. A good pimiento-cheese sandwich has a spread of mayonnaise on both sides. For those with a penchant for fat, spread a thin coat of unsalted butter and then a little mayonnaise on all your finger sandwiches. Then place a damp tea towel over them to prevent them from drying out (all this before the advent of Tupperware). I've had delicious pimiento cheese straight from the Cuisinart, but, again as with eggs, it's good to put the pimiento cheese in the fridge to allow the ingredients to mingle. Pimiento cheese comes in two textures—creamy and fluffy.

Sharp cheese is preferred for pimiento cheese. However, some cooks prefer rat cheese—yes, I've heard it spoken of that way all my life. It's a rather mild and bland American cheese, sometimes called red rind or hoop cheese. The PC recipe that makes us drool is a savory one that uses beer cheese.

Beer–Cheese Pimiento

Ingredients
8 ounces grated extra-sharp cheese
8 ounces red rind cheese or mild
    American cheese, grated
2 cloves fresh garlic
1 ½ tablespoons Worcestershire sauce
    (Lea & Perrins)
½ tablespoon salt
½ tablespoon dry mustard
½ cup beer, not "lite"
several splashes of Tabasco
1 small jar (2 ounces) diced pimientos
homemade mayonnaise to taste and to
    make a spreadable PC
¼ cup pistachio nuts—or more to taste

Using a food processor, blend the above ingredients. I add the pistachios last, as I prefer them not to be pulverized. Chill. This always improves with age.

Makes one quart.

Creamy Pimiento Cheese

Ingredients

8 ounces extra-sharp cheese, grated
8 ounces Velveeta cheese
½ cup homemade mayonnaise
½ teaspoon Tabasco sauce
¼ cup finely chopped onions
1 teaspoon Worcestershire sauce (Lea & Perrins)
1 jar (2 ounces) minced pimientos, drained
¼ cup chopped pecans, optional

Blend in food processor. Chill.

Makes two cups.

Sweet Fluffy Pimiento Cheese

Ingredients
8 ounces extra-sharp cheddar cheese
1 jar (2 ounces) diced pimientos, drained
3 tablespoons Hellmann's mayonnaise
1 tablespoon sugar

Grate cheese. Add drained pimientos to cheese and mix lightly. Add mayonnaise and sugar to mixture. With the whisk attachment, mix on high speed in the bowl of your mixer. Stop and scrape the sides, and continue on high speed until you get a very fluffy, light mixture. You can double this recipe.

Makes two+ cups.

Ann Shackelford's Savory PC

Homemade mayonnaise ingredients

1 whole egg

4 tablespoons—any combination of cider vinegar
   and/or fresh lemon juice

1 ½ cup vegetable oil, nothing fancy

¼ teaspoon salt

¼ teaspoon cayenne pepper

Pimiento cheese ingredients

1 pound rat cheese (red rind, hoop,
   or mild American), grated

half the mayonnaise above, or enough
   to bind the mixture

2 jars (2 ounces each drained) diced pimientos

grated onion to taste

Parmesan cheese to taste (at least ¼ cup, but not
   enough to overwhelm the cheese)

Mix well and chill.

Makes three cups.

Hot Pimiento Cheese with Bacon

This recipe was written by a cross-section of Delta "girls." The distinctive ingredient, Durkee Famous Sauce, is a sprightly cross between mustard and mayonnaise. We'd gladly eat paper if it was spread with Durkee's, though we prefer it on tomatoes fresh from the garden.

Ingredients
- 1 cup grated sharp cheese
- 1 tablespoon minced onion
- 1 teaspoon Worcestershire sauce (Lea & Perrins)
- ½ teaspoon Tabasco
- 2 tablespoons homemade mayonnaise
- 3 tablespoons Durkee Famous Sauce

Mix the above, spread on buttered bread, and broil or toast in oven. A few pieces of crumbled bacon on top will enhance the flavor. We keep this in the icebox and sometimes serve with cocktails.

Makes two cups.

Just One More PC

Ingredients

1 large jar (4 ounces) diced pimientos, drained
½ bottle Durkee Famous Sauce
2 cups mayonnaise
1 tablespoon dry mustard
1 teaspoon Worcestershire sauce (Lea & Perrins)
2 tablespoons lemon juice
1 ½ teaspoons cayenne pepper
3 cloves crushed garlic
2 pounds sharp cheese, grated

Mash pimientos and add all ingredients except cheese. Mix well. In the bowl of your mixer or food processor, combine this mixture and grated cheese and beat on high until blended.

This PC will keep a long time—good to have on hand for last minute use.

Makes one quart.

The Eternal Slick Ham Platter . . . and How to Make It Presentable

You'll need . . .
good lettuce (not Iceberg)
good bread
homemade mayonnaise
mustard (not French's!)
homemade pickles
homemade relish

Some dear soul, bless her heart, inevitably sends a deli platter from the supermarket—a medley of slick (deli-sliced) ham, turkey, and slices of cheese that are so chummy with each other that they're stuck together.

The deli platter reminds us of the displays in the appliance department at the old Sears, Roebuck and Company on Washington Avenue—you opened a fridge and there was an abundance of faux food.

With the right condiments and decorations a ho-hum platter of slick ham can be made quite presentable. The first step is to remove the meats and cheese slices from the plastic platter and arrange them on something nicer. Don't forget to pry the cheese slices apart! Covering the edges of the plastic tray with a nice lettuce is another trick. If the only greens and bread in the house are iceberg lettuce and gummy white bread, some sweet friend of the family can go to the market.

In the Restorative Cocktail chapter, note the recipe for marinated olives, and the Who Died? chapter has recipes for stuffed eggs. Both olives and eggs enhance a less-than-perfect platter. Southern cooks often have homemade pickles and relishes, along with homemade mustard and mayonnaise, already in their iceboxes. These, too, help perk up the platter.

A few always-useful condiments:
    Pickled Figs
    Harley's Pickles
    Spicy Mayonnaise
    Little Hebe's Jerusalem Artichoke Relish
    Tomato Chutney

Recipes follow

Pickled Figs

Ingredients

6 pounds figs (peaches or pears can also be used)
1 clove per piece of fruit
2 cups apple cider vinegar
6 cups sugar
1 piece of cinnamon stick 2 inches long

Leaving figs whole, insert one clove in each piece of fruit. (if using peaches or pears, remove the pits and halve or quarter larger fruit.)

In a large non-aluminum pot, combine vinegar and sugar. Bring to a boil, stirring until all sugar has completely dissolved. Add the cinnamon stick. Add the fruit and boil until tender. Do not let the fruit approach getting mushy.

Transfer to sterilized jars, being sure to include some juice with the fruit. Refrigerate.

Makes about a dozen half-pint jars.

Harley's Pickles

Ingredients
    1 gallon jar large sour pickles
    1 box whole peppercorns
    10 garlic cloves, peeled
    8 sticks cinnamon
    5 pounds sugar
    1 quart vinegar

Drain juice from pickles. Slice pickles into rather thick rounds and place them in a crock or large stainless container. Sprinkle peppercorns, garlic, and cinnamon sticks over pickles.

Bring the sugar and vinegar to a boil. Pour over the pickle mixture. Cover and let sit overnight.

Put in sterilized jars and refrigerate.

Spicy Mayonnaise

Ingredients

2 eggs
2 cups vegetable oil
2 tablespoons lemon juice
1 teaspoon Tabasco
$\frac{1}{2}$ teaspoon salt
$\frac{1}{2}$ teaspoon white pepper
1 heaping teaspoon Dijon mustard
1 bunch of green onions, some tops (sliced)
1 pod of garlic, minced
1 tablespoon unsalted butter

In a food processor, briefly mix the eggs. Slowly add oil. When the mixture has thickened, add lemon juice, Tabasco, salt, pepper, and mustard. Pulse to mix.

Sauté the onions and garlic in melted butter until soft. Drain and pat dry. Add to the mayonnaise mixture in the processor bowl, and pulse to mix. Correct the seasoning and chill.

Makes about two cups.

Little Hebe's Jerusalem Artichoke Relish

Do not take this relish lightly. Making it is a two-day procedure that Hebe and her father—who learned the recipe from a dear friend of Hebe's fabled aunt, Hebe, Cornell Allen—used to undertake together. Still, this relish is well worth the trouble—it's delicious and plentiful. Hebe, of course, refuses to make it unless she can pick the Jerusalem artichokes herself from her brother's yard.

Ingredients

2 to 3 quarts chopped Jerusalem artichokes
(chop and then measure)
1 quart yellow onions
2 small cabbages
1 bunch celery
2 large bell peppers
1 ½ quarts water
1 cup salt
1 ½ quarts plus ½ quart white vinegar
1 cup flour
3 heaping tablespoons French's yellow mustard
5 cups sugar
5 teaspoons turmeric
2 tablespoons mustard seeds
2 tablespoons celery seeds
1 quart dill pickles, drained and chopped

Use an enameled stockpot for this recipe. Do not use a food processor—chopping by hand is a necessity.

Soak the artichokes overnight to clean them. Be careful to remove all grit.

Coarsely chop the onions, cabbages, celery, and bell peppers. Soak them in the water, to which you have added the salt. Allow to sit overnight. Drain well the next morning.

Mix ½ quart of vinegar and flour to make a paste. Mix 1 ½ quarts vinegar with the yellow mustard. Mix together the sugar, turmeric, mustard seeds, and celery seeds, and bring to a boil. Add the vinegar/flour paste slowly, stirring constantly. Boil 3 minutes, or until thickened.

Add the drained artichokes (from yesterday) and the dill pickles. Bring to a boil and stir for 1 minute.

Put in sterilized jars and seal.

Makes 16 pints.

NOTE: Your house will smell like a hot-dog stand for two days. You should feel like a Christian martyr after making this.

Tomato Chutney

This recipe came from Madhur Jaffrey via George Shackelford. Chutney is not new to the South. We just call it a version of chow-chow. The BEST.

Ingredients

4 whole heads of garlic, peeled and coarsely chopped

4 pieces of fresh ginger, 2 or 3 inches long, peeled and coarsely chopped (use your food processor)

6 cups wine vinegar

4 (1-pound, 12-ounce) cans whole peeled tomatoes

6 cups granulated sugar

6 teaspoons salt

8 tablespoons golden raisins

8 tablespoons blanched slivered almonds

2 teaspoons cayenne pepper

Put the garlic, ginger, and 3 cups of the vinegar into the bowl of your food processor (you may have to do this a half at a time) and blend until smooth. In a large nonmetallic container, add the tomatoes, the balance of the vinegar, sugar, and salt. Bring to a boil. Add the puree from the food processor. Simmer gently, uncovered, for several hours or until thick enough to coat a spoon. Stir frequently . . . more so toward the end of the cooking process.

After the desired consistency is reached and while the chutney is hot, add raisins, almonds, and cayenne pepper. Cook 5 or 10 more minutes, stirring.

Allow to cool and then store in glass jars. Refrigerate.

This keeps for six months.

4

I Was So Embarrassed
I Liketa Died

 Some people say that funerals are for the living. This is a point of view that can be carried too far. Indeed, there is such a thing as the living having *too* much fun at a funeral. When planning or attending a funeral, one of the things to keep in mind is: Unlike the dead person, you will awaken and rise in the morning. You don't want to have been so bad you wish you could switch places with the deceased.

You don't, in short, want to be so embarrassed you liketa died.

A lot of people go around saying that they want their friends to have a good time when they die. Mrs. Filson Jessup never expressed such a wish. She was a dignified grandmother whose idea of cussing up a storm was saying, "Oh, horse feathers!" Like many older ladies in the Delta, Mrs. Jessup had absorbed the notion (while "studying" at Ward-Belmont, a now-defunct school for proper young women in Nashville, Tennessee) that going outside the house without a hat and gloves is one step away from going to the Stareka Grocery naked.

Planning Mrs. Jessup's funeral did not call for creativity. She was the sort of old lady who had never in her life sung a hymn not found in the 1940 Anglican hymnal. She never suspected that there were other kinds of religious music. That is why the Mount Bethel Struttin' Gospel Choir was perhaps not an entirely appropriate musical choice for her funeral. It would have been perfect for many people—just not Mrs. Jessup. She might also have regarded the eight or nine flashy limos, rented by her son-in-law Cooter, as more suitable for a Mafia don than herself. But the situation deteriorated further.

When you walked in the front door after the funeral, the first thing you heard was Speed McNeil, a mover and shaker in the little theater set, banging out boogie-woogie on the piano. It felt like party time. If it hadn't been for the general atmosphere of festivity, Sis McGee might have had the presence of mind to ask for something appropriate, such as a glass of white wine. She might even have had the good sense to request a Coca-Cola (pronounced "co-cola"), which in the South means any soft drink, even if it's a Pepsi or a 7-Up, though it is disloyal to your Southern roots to drink anything other than real Cokes. Coca-Cola is our national drink, and there are ladies who would lie down and die if they couldn't have one promptly at 10 in the morning. A family in Clarksdale, Mississippi, actually serves Coke at breakfast. We never say soda or pop, by the way—that's the way Yankees talk. Anyway, Sis didn't ask for a sensible white wine or Co-Cola. She allowed as how vodka and water with a twist would be nice.

Sue Ellen Potts, known in the Delta as "the Handmaiden of the Bereaved" because she always shows up and takes over (or tries to) when there is a death, volunteered to fix Sis's toddy (we call all alcoholic beverages toddies; a specifically medicinal alcoholic beverage is "a toddy for the body"). The Handmaiden is too vain to put on her glasses, so she didn't have an inkling that the pair of cut-glass decanters she poured from contained vodka and gin, not vodka and water. "This is the best drink I ever had," Sis averred appreciatively. In the Delta, too, when somebody's drink runs low, people of Mrs. Filson Jessup's generation liked to say, "Let me put a patch on that drink."

The Handmaiden put about three patches on Sis's drink, and then Sis rolled off the sofa and lay in a stupor on the Aubusson. Looking possibly worse for wear than Mrs. Jessup did at this point, Sis was carried out, feet first, by Big Cooter and Little Cooter. Her motionless body was borne right past Miss Carrie Bell, a spinster, whose eyes were out on stems.

Your emotions will do funny things at a funeral. You may not even have any emotions. But you can still have grace. A funeral reception is not a cocktail party. We want people to feel comfortable, but we want them to remember that they're there because someone has died. We take the food not because we regard death as the chance to throw a wingding—at least not officially—but because we want to express our sympathy, comfort the afflicted, and perhaps lessen the burden of having to feed out-of-town mourners who have descended upon the family to pay their last respects.

One thing we know from funerals past: You're going to get some food you don't want. Food snobs have reached the point that they're horrified at anything that comes out of a can or box. It has to be hummingbird's tongue on toast or nothing. But it's better to receive a Twinkie pie graciously than to dine haughtily on hummingbird's tongue. To their credit, even food snobs seem to drop their pretentions at funerals. They probably go into secret Jell-O withdrawal between funerals. As for the congealed salad made with Coca-Cola, you may think it should be hidden behind the epergne, but the little old ladies and gentlemen appreciate soft foods. They will be grateful for the Bing cherry salad with Coca-Cola. We don't want to go out of this world with ribs or hot 'n' spicy barbecue, but if some kindly person shows up with them, our descendants will accept them graciously. If not, we'll haunt them.

There are people in the Delta who are greatly admired because they always do or say the right thing. One such paragon is Mrs. Lassiter Pierce. We always say how much we admire her because she always holds her head up high, even though her mother ran away with the lion tamer in a traveling circus. Despite the lion-tamer taint, she has always been a lady.

Mrs. Minor Millsaps was another Delta paragon. During the legendary 1927 flood, when the Mississippi River overflowed its banks, the future Mrs. Minor Millsaps was a little girl. She found herself on a boat that was crowded with lesser mortals. "Ada," her mother famously ordered, "hold your head up high. Give the people courage." (She of course meant the common people, but Delta ladies of past generations couldn't bring themselves to let that particular word pass their lips. They said "K.O.M." instead.) Ada held her head up high, and we feel certain that everybody on the boat felt much better. Mrs. Millsaps would never have been rude to an inferior, even if confronted by a mound of hot 'n' spicy pork at her own funeral reception, which is precisely what happened.

A well-meaning local grocer, unaware of the finer points of etiquette that dictate that hot tamales and barbecue are funeral no-no's, generously sent the Millsaps enough spicy pig to feed the barbarian hordes. The Millsaps were not expecting barbarians. This did not give them an excuse to act like barbarians themselves. Lesser people would not have had the courage to do what the Millsaps family did. Holding her head up high, Betsy Minor Millsaps Miller put the ribs in a place of honor, alongside the aspic, the dainty homemade rolls, and Aunt Hebe's coconut cake. She even put the Tabasco on the table, just in case the pork wasn't hot enough for somebody, which was highly unlikely. "Mother would have died," she giggled to Tottie Taylor. But mother would have been much more mortified if her daughter had failed to accept a gift with grace.

When Mildred Boatwright died, it looked as if things

would go off without a hitch. Her nieces were worried about one thing only: The Handmaiden's fiendish fondness for napkins that were formerly trees. She'll sniff out your paper napkins with the tacky little cocktail glasses on them faster than a pig snuffling for truffles. Since the Handmaiden was Mildred's sister-in-law, it was expected that she would feature herself in an even larger role than usual, if that's possible. "We do not want Mildred to go under with paper napkins," a niece stated. In her single-minded determination to protect Mildred from one form of shame, she forgot another: She neglected to remind the family that getting knee-walking drunk and eating every last morsel of food are not the done things.

Roberta Shaw was the designated paper-napkin pooper. She was to leave the funeral early to beat the Handmaiden to the house. Unfortunately, when Roberta arrived, the fine linen napkins were just about the only items in the general vicinity of the kitchen that hadn't been eaten. You know how liquor makes you hungry? It can really wreck a diet. The Boatwright house is smack-dab in the middle of a cotton field, and Roberta couldn't just zip over to the deli and pick up a plate of slick ham with some French's mustard on the side, which would have looked mighty good right about then. The saving grace is that when people are drinking their sorrow away, they don't bother with the sweets.

So, while the aspics, homemade mayonnaise, tenderloin, and rolls were but distant memories in throbbing heads, beautiful cakes and pies had survived the grief-stricken feasting of the night. A smoked salmon had also been hidden in the hall closet, but Roberta knew that without divine intervention this fish wasn't going to go far. It is fortunate that Roberta knew how to swing in to "ruler of the kitchen" mode. After brewing several pots of coffee and decorously arranging the sweets on the sideboard with fresh flowers, she acted as if from the start she had planned a sweets-only reception. Miss Carrie Bell—who'd skipped breakfast in anticipation of the funeral meats—was openly hostile. Her stomach had been growling in church. But everyone else had a lively—or at least a sedate but pleasant—time.

An indispensable tip on how to host the perfect Southern funeral: If your family is prone to fall in the bottle at times of trial (and even if they aren't), it is recommended that you appoint somebody bossy to run the kitchen. She's most often the best friend of the lady of the house, and her word is law. You must be afraid to cross her. She will list the casseroles and aspics as they arrive, and she also will keep track of the dishes and return them to their owners within a few days of the funeral.

Ralph Highsmith's funeral was one of the more memorable, and, as in the case of Mrs. Filson Jessup's, there are a number of don'ts to be derived from it. Ralph loved romancing the ladies. Marriage did not deter him. His most famous lady friend was Earline, a part-time waitress, who had an annoying habit of galloping across the Highsmith yard on her horse during dinner. It was difficult to just ignore this. Lavinia Highsmith divorced Ralph when she couldn't stand it another minute. So we were surprised when Lavinia announced that she would attend Ralph's funeral. But we knew she wasn't kidding when she moved up her regular Botox appointment and went shopping for something nice to wear. No ex-wife cares to be outshone by her successor.

Ralph's obsequies were to be in a small town several hours from Greenville, where he had spent his sunset years with Earline. To arrive in style, Lavinia hired a King Air, which is just a cut below the executive jet. The King Air is the plane of choice for the Delta's jet set. This is because flying in a King Air is even more fun than staying in the car while it goes through the scrub brushes at the U-Serve Car Wash on Highway 82, a pastime we often describe as being "more fun than a barrel of monkeys." With a King Air, you can let your friends know you're coming by buzzing them. Buzzing occurs when you risk your life by flying dangerously low, and it is considered a form of witticism in the Mississippi Delta. This is one of the many fascinating things you can do if you live where there are no tall buildings to get in the way. Another attractive feature of the King Air is that you can make it wave hello and good-bye with its wings. We aren't sure that the regional aeronautics authorities are as enthusiastic about these attributes as we are.

Lavinia was running so late that she asked the pilot to please swoop down so she could see if people were already arriving for the service. Unfortunately, they were. The plane buzzed the church so loud that we wondered if the racket was going to wake Ralph. A few minutes later, Lavinia—the only living soul in the Ark-La-Miss, if not the entire planet, unaware of the havoc she had just wreaked—strolled serenely into the church. She was wearing her Christian martyr facial expression and a drop-dead gorgeous pair of black designer slacks. "I don't want anybody to know I'm here," she stage-whispered. "I'm just here for the children."

As you already see, there were just a lot of don'ts at Ralph Highsmith's funeral. And we haven't even gotten to the music yet. . . . It is *never* a good idea to choose a hymn with a lot of high notes. Baby Doll Highsmith, who despite her name is in her forties, laughed so hard when a large lady in an ostrich-feathered hat hit a high note that—well, a lady will refrain from going into details. You can't go wrong with the old standards, like "Oh, God, Our Help in Ages Past." This will work well for almost anybody but the most out-and-out atheist. Sarah Benedict wanted to sing "Now Thank We All Our God" at her mother's funeral. But somebody prevailed upon her to make another selection, because Sarah's mother—who was hyper-sensitive and had no sense of humor whatsoever—might take it the wrong way. Sarah did a quick flip-flop to "A Mighty Fortress Is Our God."

Speed McNeil loved Barbra Streisand. When his wife died, we were stunned by his sudden, tragic loss; we were more stunned when Mary Ellen Hookis—she had starred in the popular little theater production of *Funny Girl*—stepped out from under the tent and meaningfully cleared her throat. The next thing we heard was: "Funny, did you hear that? Funny! Yeah, the guy said, 'Honey, you're a funny girl.'" We were so embarrassed we liketa died.

Funny Girl wasn't the only wretched excess. When Speed emerged from his toilette for the solemn ride to the church, he looked like he'd been hanging crepe—on himself. He was wearing a black Miss America-style sash under his coat. We asked him if it was some mourning custom we didn't know. He said no, he just liked it. He added that he thought it made him look dignified, but he was the only one who held that opinion. Sartorial eccentricities are to be eschewed at a funeral, especially by members of the immediate family.

Sometimes, though, breaking the rules just seems right—it all depends on who is being buried. Not just anybody can carry off being buried to the accompaniment of a foghorn. But one local woman did. At her graveside, her husband—like his wife, a local history and Delta lore buff—chose to read a poem about the Mississippi River. Whenever he got to the refrain about *moooournful* foghorns blowing on the river, the owner of a towboat company—he was hiding behind the bushes—blew a *looong* blast on a foghorn. It was an authentic foghorn from one of his tugboats. We might also mention that her husband asked a friend to sit by her coffin and sing and play the guitar all night.

A champagne toast—and then several more champagne toasts—followed the foghorn. Before you knew it, everybody was singing and dancing and crying and laughing. They were also throwing gifts into the grave. "You always loved this," sobbed her best friend, throwing her expensive pashmina shawl into the grave. The desire to give was contagious, but it is not true that somebody sobered up the next day to find his Rolex missing. No doubt, this grave will one day prove an interesting dig for archeologists studying Delta funerary customs.

After the grave, there was peel-'em-and-eat-'em shrimp. Hardly your proper Delta funeral fare, but the whole event was filled with love. The grieving husband even thought to ask St. James' to toll the bell once for every year of his wife's life. Of course, in the interest of chivalry, we trust he knocked off a few years.

Leland Grits Gruyere

There's nothing better than taking a big vat of grits to some-body's house. I don't know if cheese grits really do help soak up excess alcohol, but this recipe is certainly comforting. Grits is a comfort food, great for breakfast or lunch. This recipe is quite similar to one in Memphis's popular *Potpourri* cookbook, but with some variations introduced by the McGee family of Leland, Mississippi. A word on grits: There are three kinds of grits on the market. One kind, instant grits, is not like grits at all. You might as well be eating cream of wheat. Quick grits are all right. The best is coarsely ground grits.

Ingredients
   1 quart milk
   ½ cup butter
   1 cup coarsely ground grits (not instant)
   1 teaspoon salt
   1 teaspoon white pepper
   ⅓ cup butter
   5 ounces grated Gruyere cheese
   ¾ cup grated Parmesan cheese

Preheat the oven to 350°.

Bring the milk to a boil and add ½ cup butter.

Add the grits. Stir constantly for about 5 minutes, or until the grits are thick. Remove the pan from the heat. Add salt and pepper to taste. Beat well, with an egg beater. Add ⅓ cup butter and Gruyere cheese. Pour into a greased 2-quart casserole and bake for a half hour. Remove from oven and sprinkle with Parmesan cheese. Continue to bake for another thirty minutes. Allow to sit for a few minutes before serving.

Serves eight to ten.

Vodka Cake

We're embarrassed to death to tell you what's in this cake. It sounds downright trashy. How many of the world's great chefs use Jell-O pudding? This recipe also calls for store-bought icing. But it's simply one of the best things you'll ever put in your mouth, and perfect for taking to the home of the bereaved. The biggest testament to this improbable recipe: Vodka Cake is all the rage at St. James' Episcopal Church, despite the church's heretofore ironclad no-store-bought-mixes dogma. But don't let the humble ingredients lull you into thinking you can get away with just any old rot-gut vodka. Gayden borrows a half cup of her husband's very best, and it makes all the difference. One of the selling points of this cake is that it stays moist forever (and ever).

We always feel better after making this cake. We wonder why.

Ingredients

    1 box Duncan Hines yellow cake mix
    1 small (3.4-ounce) box and 1 large (5.9-ounce)
       box chocolate pudding mix
    4 eggs at room temperature, beaten
    1 cup oil
    ½ cup Kahlua
    ½ cup vodka
    1 container store-bought chocolate-fudge icing

Preheat the oven to 350°.

Combine, in the bowl of your mixer, the cake mix, chocolate pudding mixes, and eggs. Mix until creamy. Add the oil, Kahlua, and vodka, and twirl around until there are no lumps. Pour into a well-oiled bundt pan (8-cup size) and bake for approximately 45 minutes. Take it out of the oven and allow it to sit a minute, and then flip it out onto the plate on which you intend to deliver it. While it is still piping hot, open the can of store-bought chocolate fudge icing and spread it on the cake. It will melt into the cake and the result is celestial. By the way, this is wonderful with home-made cinnamon ice cream, though that would be too cumbersome to transport to the bereaved.

Serves twelve

Beef Tenderloin

This is not an inexpensive dish to take, but it is easy to prepare and always the best received. Along with the rosemary new potatoes, this is standard dinner fare for the family the night before the funeral. Both dishes have the added advantage of tasting even better after being left on the sideboard for a while. This is best cooked on an outdoor grill and then cooled and wrapped in foil. With an expensive cut of meat, you might prefer simply grilling it with a little salt and lots of pepper.

Ingredients
5 to 6 pounds beef tenderloin
1 ½ sticks butter, softened
4 cloves garlic, crushed
2 teaspoons Worcestershire sauce (Lea & Perrins)
2 teaspoons lemon juice
salt
freshly ground pepper—you'll want to use
    lots of it

Preheat the oven to 500°.

Allow the tenderloin to come to room temperature.

To the softened butter, add crushed garlic, Worcestershire sauce, lemon juice, salt, and pepper. Spread this on the tenderloin.

Cook uncovered on a baking sheet for 23 minutes. Remove from oven, wrap meat in foil, and allow to rest for 20 minutes. Unwrap immediately to discontinue cooking.

Serves ten or more.

Alternative Pork Tenderloin

Southern ladies are told ne-vuh to talk about money. It's not nice. But you see, as much as we hate to bring it up, we just don't have any. We're living in the past—it makes life more charming. Our mothers would never let us eat pork in the summer. We wondered why. They were much too nice to say that they thought it would give us trichinosis. But now we have refrigeration! We also have, much as we hate to mention an unpleasant subject, beef that's far too expensive. The pork tenderloin is now very popular. If at all possible, also take along the tomato chutney (see page 97).

Ingredients
¾ cup Kikkoman teriyaki marinade
   and sauce
¼ cup bourbon
2 tablespoons brown sugar
2 garlic cloves, minced
2 pork tenderloins,
   about 1 ¾ to 2 pounds each

Mix the marinade, bourbon, sugar, and garlic thoroughly. Cover the tenderloins with the marinade. Put them in a Ziploc bag and chill for several hours or overnight, turning the bag frequently to ensure that both tenderloins are covered in marinade.

These are best grilled outside, but they can be cooked in a 400° oven for approximately 20 minutes, basting along the way.

Take the tenderloins whole, because they should not be sliced until just before serving. These make great sandwiches on homemade rolls with mayonnaise, hot mustard, and tomato chutney.

Serves eight or more.

Rosemary New Potatoes

The thing to do here is to surround the tenderloin with the new potatoes. That way, you have fewer dishes to carry (and to be returned), not to mention that it looks nice. Homemade rolls and a mozzarella-and-tomato salad are perfect with the tenderloin and rosemary potatoes for dinner for the family the night before the funeral.

Ingredients
2 pounds small red new potatoes
8 tablespoons olive oil
6 tablespoons fresh rosemary
   or 3 teaspoons dried
freshly ground pepper
salt

Cut the potatoes into quarters if they are small. Otherwise, cut them into sixths. Heat a nonstick pan and add olive oil. Add potatoes and rosemary, and reduce the heat. Toss a minute or two, cover, and cook about 10 minutes. Add pepper and salt to taste. I have used a garlic-and-herb-flavored olive oil that makes a very tasty dish.

Serves six

Mozzarella Cheese and Tomatoes

In a small town like Greenville, we don't get really good mozzarella. What we use is probably more akin to a B. F. Goodrich product than what you can get in a big city. But guess what—this is still utterly delicious. We can only imagine what it would be like with the right stuff! The beauty of this recipe is that it tastes better if it is left at room temperature for a while, which means that it doesn't have to infringe on valuable refrigerator space.

Ingredients
5 nice ripe tomatoes,
    peeled and sliced
mozzarella cheese
selected greens
freshly ground pepper
fresh basil, coarsely chopped
vinaigrette

Arrange alternating slices of tomatoes and mozzarella on a bed of selected greens. Apply freshly ground pepper and a sprinkling of coarsely chopped basil. Nap with vinaigrette.

Vinaigrette

½ cup red wine vinegar
salt and pepper to taste
1 teaspoon sugar
minced green onions or fresh chives,
    about ¼ cup (or to taste)
capers
2 tablespoons coarse mustard
    (Dijon or moutard de meau)
1 cup olive oil

Mix the vinegar, salt, pepper, sugar, onions, and capers. Add the mustard. Whisk the olive oil into the mixture slowly. Allow the dressing to rest, then whisk again and use approximately ⅛ cup—no more—on the salad. The longer this sits, the better it gets. That's my personal preference.

To peel a tomato, drop it into a pot of boiling water and remove it immediately. Rinse it in cold water. The skin will pop right off. If it is stubborn, slide the tip of a sharp knife beneath the skin and pull.

Serves six

Homemade Vegetable Soup

Southerners have a habit of leaving food out on the counter or on the back of the stove, and it hasn't killed us yet. This delicious soup is good for the grieving family—another great comfort food. Serve it with corn bread and salad.

Ingredients

butter

4 boneless, skinless chicken breasts, chicken breast tenders, or 3 pounds cubed beef

1 large or 2 medium onions, chopped

2 stalks celery, sliced

1 large can (28 ounces) diced tomatoes or chopped whole tomatoes

1 large can (14.5 ounces) tomato sauce

1 large (1 pound) package frozen mixed vegetables

1 large or 2 medium potatoes, peeled and sliced, rather chunky

3 teaspoons pepper

2 teaspoons salt

1 teaspoon dried oregano

2 ½ quarts water

Melt the butter in a large pot and brown the chicken or beef. Remove the meat, add the onions and celery, and sauté briefly. Return the meat to the pot. Add the tomatoes, tomato sauce, vegetables, seasonings, and water.

Cook several hours. Sometimes I leave it on simmer for four or five hours. This can be seasoned along the way, as can most other recipes, though I find it perfect as is. I add any fresh vegetables that I might have on hand. Butter beans, when available, are a wonderful addition.

Serves ten.

Mary Mills Abington's Chocolate Sheet Cake

The glory of this recipe is that it serves a lot of people. It is proper for the reception after the funeral or for refreshments throughout the time when friends call to pay their respects.

Ingredients

    2 cups flour
    2 cups sugar
    3 ½ tablespoons cocoa
    1 stick margarine
    1 cup water
    ½ cup Wesson oil
    2 eggs, beaten
    ½ cup buttermilk
    1 ½ teaspoons vanilla
    1 teaspoon baking soda

Preheat the oven to 350°.

Mix the flour, sugar, and cocoa in a bowl. Boil the margarine, water, and oil for 1 minute, then add to first mixture. Combine the beaten eggs with the buttermilk, vanilla, and baking soda. Beat until well mixed and add to previous mixture.

Pour onto large, greased 10 ½ x 15 x 1-inch pan. Bake for 20 minutes. Don't overcook. Keep an eye on the edges.

Frosting

- 1 stick margarine
- 3 ½ tablespoons powdered cocoa
- 1 tablespoon milk
- 1 box confectioners' sugar
- 1 ½ teaspoons vanilla
- 1 cup chopped pecans

Bring the margarine, cocoa, and milk to a boil. Add the sugar and mix well, and then add the vanilla and pecans.

Spread frosting over hot cake. Upon cooling, cut into small squares.

Makes 40 appropriately sized (that means not too big) squares.

Hardin's Hardy Potatoes

This recipe comes from Mary Lee Hardin, who is the Handmaiden of the Bereaved—the first at the house with a nice, comforting dish—of Gadsden, Alabama.

Ingredients
9 medium baking potatoes, peeled
½ stick butter
1 ½ teaspoons salt
½ teaspoon pepper
3 tablespoons chopped green onions
⅔ cup heated milk
1 cup heavy whipping cream
1 ½ cups grated cheese
Paprika

Boil the potatoes until tender. Drain, mash, and whip them with a mixer. Add the butter, salt, pepper, onions, and milk. Beat until light and fluffy. Pour into a buttered shallow baking dish (this may be done ahead of time).

Whip the cream and add the grated cheese. Spread evenly over potatoes. Sprinkle the top with paprika and bake at 350° for 25 minutes, or until golden brown.

Serves ten.

Liketa Died Potatoes

This is the last thing a snoot would take to somebody's house, but the first thing that would be eaten. I liketa died when I saw what was in this recipe. Corn flakes, hash browns, cheddar cheese soup, and sour cream—not the food-group combinations favored at the great culinary schools. But I've never seen it fail—people practically inhale Liketa Died Potatoes.

Ingredients
    1 two-pound package hash browns
    10 ounces grated sharp cheddar cheese
    ½ cup chopped onions
    1 pint sour cream
    1 can (10 ¾ ounces) cheddar cheese soup,
        not diluted
    1 teaspoon salt
    2 teaspoons pepper, coarsely ground

Topping
    2 cups corn flakes
    1 stick butter

Preheat the oven to 350°.

Prepare the hash browns according to the package directions. Combine with the other ingredients. Place in a greased, buttered, 13 x 9-inch casserole. Top the casserole with corn flakes and dot with butter. Bake for 40 minutes or until golden, crisp, and bubbly.

Serves eight.

St. James' Cranberry Congealed Salad

This salad has been served for forty-five years at the St. James' Bazaar, even though it's another one of those I-liketa-died-when-they . . . recipes. Can you imagine topping Jell-O with homemade mayonnaise? Would you waste your homemade mayonnaise that way? All I know is that it works. People eat every last morsel. Maybe they think the cranberries are good for them.

Relish
> 1 pound fresh cranberries
> 1 orange, quartered, seeded, not peeled
> 1 cup sugar

Wash berries. Grind berries with orange and sugar in the food processor.

Salad
> 1 (3-ounce) box orange Jell-O
> $\frac{1}{2}$ the amount of water called for in the Jell-O
> $\frac{1}{2}$ cup chopped celery
> $\frac{3}{4}$ cup cranberry mixture
> $\frac{1}{2}$ cup chopped pecans

Mix the Jell-O with hot water per package directions and add other ingredients. Allow to congeal. Serve topped with homemade mayonnaise.

Serves eight

Alternative Bing Cherry Congealed Salad

Ingredients
   1 large (20-ounce) can crushed pineapple
   1 (15-ounce) can bing cherries
   2 Texas ruby red grapefruits, sectioned
   1 (3-ounce) box cherry Jell-O
   1 (3-ounce) box raspberry Jell-O
   2 cups combined juice, reserved from grapefruit,
      pineapple, and cherries, heated

Dissolve the Jell-O in the hot juice. Pour it into a casserole dish.

When the Jell-O begins to get firm, fold in pineapple, cherries, and grapefruit. Chill until firm.

Serves eight.

Bing Cherry Salad with Coca-Cola

Gayden's grandmother, Annie Gayden, never learned to cook or drive—she said if you don't learn, you won't have to do either. But there was one thing she knew how to make: bing cherry salad with Coca-Cola. I think that ladies of a certain age must have believed that bing cherries were the last word in elegance. There is an entire page in one of my mother's recipe books devoted to variations on the bing cherry salad. This recipe is from *Gourmet of the Delta*. Annie Gayden insisted that only bottled Coca-Cola be used. Canned Coke is heresy.

Ingredients

2 (3-ounce) boxes cherry Jell-O
1 number-2 can (20 ounces, or 2 ½ cups)
    crushed pineapple, drained
1 number-303 can (15-ounces, or about 2 cups)
    black cherries, drained
2 cups juice (reserved from pineapple and
    cherries), heated
2 (8-ounce) bottles Coca-Cola
1 cup pecans

Dissolve the Jell-O in the hot juice, then add the Coca-Cola and pour into a dish. When Jell-O starts to congeal, stir in the pineapple, quartered cherries, and pecans. Chill until firm.

Serves sixteen.

It's Too Early to Talk Breakfast

Like Count Dracula, who was from a lovely old family, Southern ladies of a certain ilk and age only come alive at night. One or two in the morning is the normal bedtime for the night-owl belle, who tends to have attained at least her seventieth year. No, they don't prowl about the Delta seeking the restorative blood of young beaux—they sit up all night smoking cigarettes, watching TV, or drinking gin, or—if worse comes to worst—reading a book. Not all Southern ladies sit up all night, but the ones who do so regard it as a point of honor. While the rest of us are in bed getting our zzz's, the night-owl belle is flipping through her *TV Guide*, searching for *Dynasty* reruns, and not even thinking about applying her Swiss Performing lotion for another hour or so.

Southern ladies used to regard sleeping late as their prerogative. Mothers used to train their daughters to sleep late. One Southern mother, eager to pass down her traditions, would refuse to awaken her daughter for any telephone call that came in before midday. "She needs her sleep," she would say indignantly. School chums who visited from other parts of the country were invariably shocked at what they thought was a lazy and degenerate habit. We were all brought up that way, but our daughters aren't so lucky. Staying awake all night may be a habit engendered in the night-owl belle by attending endless dances and cotillions in her salad days, but it is no longer practical for most of us—it's a relic from the era when husbands would let the children starve before allowing their wives to soil their po' sweet little hands with work.

Daughters of these night-owl belles have to go to work in the morning these days. But the custom is so deeply ingrained that, now in their forties or fifties, the daughters feel they're letting down the team when they trudge off to bed at a reasonable hour. "I'm just not a lady," they sigh, as they fall into bed at 10:30. "Mama would be so ashamed."

Breakfast is never the Southern lady's favorite meal—after all, many have just gone to bed and are intent on getting their beauty rest. She is likely to be even more tired than usual if there has been a death in the family—she most likely had an especially late night, staying up to polish every bit of silver in the house. Bearing this in mind, you can't go wrong taking the bereaved family something brunchlike to eat the morning of the funeral. The ideal dish can be put in the refrigerator, reheated, and placed on the buffet for informal nibbling—even in the Delta, families no longer sit down to breakfast together. Toasted banana nut bread (recipe on page 184) is delicious, and grits (pages 110 and 164) are a great comfort, particularly when prepared simply and served with lots of butter. A big bowl of fresh fruit, a blessed relief from the abundance of funeral goo, is most welcome.

The night-owl belle, or for that matter anybody else facing a funeral, won't want to make conversation at an hour she regards as daybreak, which, roughly translated, is any time before midday. But Southerners are too polite to shoo you away. It's up to you to drop off your dish and dash. If you can leave your offering in the kitchen without even being seen, like Scarlet the Good Fairy, all the better.

Fresh Fruit

Ingredients

fresh seasonal fruits
1 can orange-juice concentrate
sliced bananas

This is such a nice thing to do because fruit is light and goes well with toast or heavier breakfast fare. It depends, of course, on what's in season. A nice combination would be: cantaloupe, blueberries, strawberries, grapes, and fresh pineapple. Slice the fruit, mix and coat it with the juice concentrate. Chill. Add sliced bananas just before serving.

Breakfast Casserole

Even breakfast brings out our inner casserole! This is an egg strata that is hearty but not too hearty (you don't want a big breakfast before a funeral).

Ingredients

butter

12 slices white bread (regular gummy white bread—nothing fancy, please)

1 pound bacon, fried

1 bunch green onions (about nine), sliced

3 cups finely shredded extra-sharp cheddar cheese

a dozen eggs, beaten

4 cups half-and-half

1 teaspoon salt

1 teaspoon white pepper

½ cup shredded Parmesan cheese

Generously butter a 9 x 13-inch baking dish. Line the bottom with 6 pieces of bread. Crumble half the cooked bacon over the bread. Sprinkle half the onions and half the cheddar cheese over the bacon. Mix the eggs, half-and-half, salt, and pepper until blended. Pour half of it evenly over the bread-cheese layers. Repeat the layering with remaining bread, bacon, onion, and cheddar cheese. Pour the remaining egg-cream mixture over the top. Sprinkle with Parmesan cheese. Cover and refrigerate overnight.

Bring casserole to room temperature.

Preheat the oven to 325°. Bake casserole uncovered for 40 minutes, or until set.

Serves ten.

Morning Glory Muffins

Bad recipe name for the day of a funeral, but the muffin is nevertheless suitable. The recipe is from Methodist stalwart Norma de Long, and so we know it's comforting. Because it contains carrots, Greenville people are somehow convinced that this is health food. Perhaps "Ode to Health Muffins" should be the name. Of course, there is that cup and a half of sugar.

Ingredients

2 cups flour
1 ½ cups sugar
2 teaspoons baking soda
2 teaspoons cinnamon
½ teaspoon salt
2 cups of grated carrots
½ cup raisins
½ cup chopped nuts
½ cup shredded coconut
1 apple, peeled, cored, and grated
3 eggs
1 cup vegetable oil
2 teaspoons vanilla

Preheat the oven to 350°.

In a large bowl, sift together the flour, sugar, baking soda, cinnamon, and salt. Stir in the grated carrots, raisins, nuts, coconut, and apple. Beat together the eggs, oil, and vanilla. Stir this into the flour mixture until just moistened. Spoon batter into well-greased muffin tins.

Bake 15 minutes and check to be sure they are firm to the touch. If you use small muffin tins, which are preferred, the time will be less.

Makes two dozen small muffins.

5

Comfort Foods:
There Is a Balm in Campbell's
Soup (sung to the tune of
"There is a Balm in Gilead")

 When Ann Dudley Whatever-Her-Last-Name-Was-at-the-Time's father, Hubert, died, Big Ann Dudley was so beside herself she nearly buried him in "the JFK." According to what Bubba Boone, our premier funeral director, told Big Ann Dudley at the time, the JFK is a deluxe, tastefully appointed coffin modeled on the very one in which President John F. Kennedy was laid to rest. (If that doesn't grab you, Bubba offers the Alma Mater—it has your college seal—or the Fan—your favorite football team's mascot—

affixed to the lid. There used to be the Last Supper, which had the scene painted on the inside of the lid so the deceased had something to look at when it was closed. (The Last Supper was exclusive to the discount coffin outlet, which went out of business.)

Coffins are so expensive nowadays, we know somebody who bought his online—he put it in the corner of the living room and tried it on for size several times. "You always want to be comfortable," he said, adding, "I plan to spend a lot of time in it."

Big Ann Dudley wasn't thinking straight, and was just about to sign on the dotted line when Little Ann Dudley arrived, just in the nick of time. "Mama," she wailed, "you can't put Daddy in the JFK. He was a devoted Republican." A few seconds later, and the chairman of the county Republicans would have found himself in the JFK.

Buddy Gilliam was buried in the "Old Miss," but his daughter was so distressed that she almost forgot to make good on a death-bed promise: Mr. Buddy refused to die until she agreed to pin a note to his lapel that said, "Hell, no, I don't look nachell." Making somebody promise to pin a "Hell, no, I don't look nachell." note on your dead body is the Delta version of a living will—it tells you how we want to be disposed of and must be obliged. Old ladies are inclined to chat endlessly about what they want to wear in their coffins and threaten to return and haunt their friends if their instructions aren't carried out to the letter. "Once you're in heaven, do you get stuck in the clothes you're buried in?" asked one of our more vain little old ladies. Of course, no matter what you end up wearing, we will say, "Doesn't she look natural?"—even if you've been got up to look like Barbie in a coffin.

Sarah Jones's Aunt Bitsy must have looked decidedly "unnachell." Even the family noticed. She was one of Bubba's rare aesthetic failures. The relatives were hovering around Bitsy's coffin murmuring about how it just "didn't look a thing in the world like Bitsy." "Well, I guess not," harrumphed Sarah. "She's *dead*." You must be prepared for people to say strange things when they are grief stricken. Of course, Sarah always was a killjoy, and besides she and Bitsy hadn't spoken a word to each other since they had the big falling out over who was entitled to the back pew on the left-hand side at St. James'. Sarah looked like the cat that swallowed the canary when she waltzed into church the next Sunday.

A sudden loss always reminds you why you are glad you don't live in some big metropolis. People in small towns instinctively want to help each other through a crisis. In good times, you're always complaining that everybody knows your business. In bad times, you know that the covered dishes are on the way. The smaller the town, the more food you will get. They say it's more fattening to lose a relative in Alligator or Hushpuckena than it is in Jackson or Vicksburg.

Nobody in the world eats better than the bereaved Southerner. In the Delta, we ask not for whom the bell tolls— it tolls for all of us, and the message we hear is "Open a can of Campbell's cream of mushroom soup and get busy." "When somebody dies, I may not know them well enough to go to the house or attend the funeral," said one Delta cook, "but I can always take the family a cake or casserole."

While we celebrate weddings, christenings, birthdays, and other milestones with food, everybody knows that death cooking is our very best. When Nellia Bostwick's husband Andrew died in California, she said that the worst thing about it was missing all the good cooking—and missing Andy, too, of course. Southern funeral food won't bring back the dead—in fact, it's so rich it may be food to die *from*.

Delta funeral cooking is two-tiered—there's the *haute* funeral food, which includes aspics, homemade mayonnaise, and dainty homemade rolls. The second tier is dishes that are Campbell's soup based. Methodist cooking—with its strong reliance on cream of mushroom soup—falls into this category. Velveeta cheese, almond slivers, French-fried (canned) onions, and Ritz crackers are other defining ingredients. If you go too long without a funeral, your body may go into "goo withdrawal syndrome."

Whenever you mix high-carbohydrate anything with Velveeta or mushroom soup, you will produce a dish guaranteed to bring comfort. Food is grief therapy in the Delta. Nothing whispers sympathy quite like a frozen-pea casserole with canned bean sprouts and mushroom soup. If you've been away awhile, it may sound like an odd recipe. "Who on earth brought this?" asked a food snob who'd been living elsewhere for too long. "I did," her mother said. "Well, Mama, don't you ever stop," she said before digging into the pea casserole. Would you really prefer the upscale white sauce and Swiss

cheese with almonds to the traditional can of cream of mushroom soup, cheddar cheese, and french-fried onions? 'Taint
much difference in the taste department, but Campbell's is
more consoling. "Carb therapy" may kill us in the long run, but
we feel that these foods soak up the alcohol and give us the
energy to do what we know we have to do.

An outsider might think that small-town food is fresh
food. But this is not the case—at least not at funerals. A cardinal rule of Southern funeral cooking: Fresh is not best. A leafy
green salad just doesn't seem right when someone has died.
Sarah Jones thought her niece, who'd come from California for
Aunt Bitsy's funeral, was just about the rudest person she'd
ever met because she failed to grasp this basic rule. The niece
not only talked like a Yankee, she said she'd eaten enough
Velveeta and mushroom soup to last her until her own funeral.
She said she wanted a Cobb salad. A *Cobb* salad? When somebody has *died*? Frankly, none of us could believe our ears.
Sarah wrote her niece out of her will. Somebody so un-
Southern wouldn't have the foggiest notion what to do with
family silver.

When you examine the cream-of-mushroom situation,
you'll find that the farther out in the country you are, the
more of it you see. Unlike Sarah's rude niece, we know that no
matter what kind of garden you have, you just don't take a festive basket of fresh corn when somebody has died. Many
Delta cooks keep their pantries stocked with staples to prepare
funeral-appropriate dishes. This is the culinary equivalent of
making sure to have a summer and a winter funeral frock

hanging in the closet at all times. The freezer and the can-stocked pantry are to Southern funeral food what the whisk and mold were to Brillat-Savarin, the great French gastrono-mist, who once said, "Tell me what you eat, and I will tell you what you are." It's a pretty safe bet that nobody ever replied, "Green-bean casserole with Campbell's soup and onion rings fresh from the can." He didn't know what he was missing. Poor thing. Or, as we say in the Delta, Po' thing.

The Crocheted-Bedpan-Award Chicken

Southern girls are never supposed to mention the "B" room. This starts in first grade, when we quietly ask the teacher if we may go to the "basement." Of course, if there were a basement in the Delta, it would be three feet deep in water. We have always eschewed "B"-room talk. Our friend Charlotte McGee said that when she was a little girl she asked her mother how the commode (Southern for "toilet") worked. Big Charlotte turned ashen. She recovered and explained that little angels from heaven came down with pink velvet bags and whisked it all away. Is it any wonder we'd all be in therapy if we had enough shrinks down here? Nonetheless, at age fifty, we still say we are going to powder our nose. You will definitely want to powder your nose if you eat (or rather imbibe) this rich chicken. This is a recipe that was developed from another chicken recipe known as Death by Chicken. It was named DBC because you could put this dish in the oven before you left for the funeral service and—*viola!*—when you returned, it was ready, just in time for the bereaved. We feel this is very upscale because it uses cream of asparagus soup rather than cream of mushroom.

Ingredients

6 slices uncooked bacon
10 chicken breast tenderloins
1 cup uncooked instant brown rice
1 can (10 ¾-ounces) cream of asparagus soup
   (actually, cream of anything will work)
1 teaspoon basil
1 teaspoon oregano
grating of fresh nutmeg
salt and pepper
sprinkling of cayenne pepper

Preheat the oven to 300°.

Cover the bottom of a 9 x 13-inch baking dish with
bacon. Put the chicken tenderloins on top of the bacon.
Pour the rice evenly over the chicken. Mix one cup of
water with the canned soup. To this mixture add basil,
oregano, and nutmeg, and pour it over the chicken.
Sprinkle with salt, pepper, and cayenne. Cover the dish
with aluminum foil and bake for 90 minutes. This
should be taken cooked to the bereaved. . . . You can't
take a casserole that requires an hour and a half to cook
as an offering.

Serves eight.

Mama, Don't Ever Stop Making Yo' Green Pea Casserole

Sure, this uses fresh mushrooms, but one fresh item isn't enough to overcome the mushroom soup, frozen peas, and canned sprouts that make this a dish to die *from*. It'll be a blissful way to go.

Ingredients

   2 (10-ounce) packages frozen peas,
      thawed
   2 (10 ¾-ounce) cans mushroom soup
   1 (12-ounce) can bean sprouts, rinsed
      and drained
   1 (8-ounce) can sliced water chestnuts
   ½ pound fresh mushrooms, sliced
   3 tablespoons butter
   salt and pepper
   1 teaspoon lemon juice
   1 teaspoon soy sauce
   1 (2-ounce) package slivered almonds

Preheat the oven to 350°.

Gently mix the peas, soup, bean sprouts, and water chestnuts. Sauté the mushrooms in 2 tablespoons butter about 3 minutes, or until the mushrooms begin to release the butter. Fold the mushrooms into the pea mixture. Season with salt, pepper, lemon juice, and soy sauce.

With the remaining tablespoon of butter, grease a 2-quart casserole, pour in the mixture, and top with almonds. Bake 30 minutes or until bubbling hot.

Serves eight.

Asparagus Casserole

This used to be a Thanksgiving and Christmas staple. But now that we've all been to culinary classes and tried to upscale our ways, this casserole has been relegated to the funeral-food buffet. Its history as a holiday food would ordinarily render it too festive for somber occasions. But we love it so much we can't give it up, and we know that funerals cry out for canned asparagus.

Ingredients
    4 (15-ounce) cans whole green asparagus
    4 tablespoons butter
    4 tablespoons flour
    2 cups milk
    2 cups grated extra-sharp cheese
    $\frac{1}{2}$ teaspoon salt
    $\frac{1}{2}$ teaspoon Tabasco
    white pepper
    4 hard-boiled eggs, peeled and sliced
    1 cup slivered almonds, toasted
    buttered bread crumbs

Preheat the oven to 350°.

Drain the asparagus. Make a white sauce using butter, flour, and milk. Add the grated cheese. Season with salt, Tabasco, and white pepper. Place a layer of asparagus in a deep dish, cover with sauce, a layer of sliced eggs, and a sprinkling of sliced almonds. Repeat the layering. Top with buttered bread crumbs. Bake until brown and bubbling. Let this sit a few minutes before serving.

Serves eight.

Tomato Soup Salad

Do Yankees eat Tomato Soup Salad? I bet they don't, po' things. Tomato Soup Salad may be regarded as the comfort-food rendering of the more exalted aspic. But it's not either or: You *must* have aspic, and it's nice to have this in addition. Our older ladies are especially devoted to Tomato Soup Salad, but they would be doubly bereaved if they didn't also find aspic.

Ingredients
    2 packages Knox unflavored gelatin
    2 (10 ¾-ounce) cans tomato soup
    2 small (3-ounce) packages cream cheese, softened
    1 cup mayonnaise (store-bought okay)
    1 cup chopped celery
    1 cup chopped olives
    white pepper

Dissolve the gelatin in ½ cup water. Heat the soup and add the dissolved gelatin.

Remove the pan from the stove. Add the cream cheese, mayonnaise, celery, and olives. This will be a somewhat lumpy mixture. You do not want it to be a purée. Pour it into a 9 × 9 × 2-inch pan that has been lightly coated with mayonnaise. Refrigerate until firm. Of course, you want to serve each square with a dollop of mayo.

Serves eight.

Tomato Pie

Another comfort food that requires store-bought mayonnaise. But don't let commercial mayonnaise become a habit.

Ingredients
    2 cups Bisquick
    ½ cup milk
    3 large (or 4 medium) fresh tomatoes
    1 cup Hellmann's mayonnaise
    ½ cup grated extra-sharp
      cheddar cheese
    salt
    coarsely ground black pepper
    ½ teaspoon basil
    1 teaspoon fresh lemon juice

Preheat the oven to 350°.

Make a pie crust using the Bisquick and milk (this fills a 9-inch pie pan). Peel and core the tomatoes. Slice them and fill the pie shell. Combine the mayonnaise and shredded cheese. Add salt, pepper, basil, and lemon juice. Spread over the tomatoes. Add an extra sprinkle of fresh pepper.

This pie puffs . . . Do not fill your pie shell too full.
Bake for 30 to 40 minutes, or until bubbly and brown.

Serves eight.

*NOTE: If you like curry, you can
add a teaspoon to the mayo mixture.*

Broccoli Squares

We serve this broccoli at St. James' for the church bazaar, but it's also funeral approved. A reminder that death brings out the yearning for funeral goo.

Ingredients
2 cups cooked broccoli, mashed
1 cup Kraft mayonnaise
1 cup evaporated milk
3 eggs, well beaten
1 tablespoon butter
1 teaspoon flour
$\frac{1}{2}$ teaspoon salt
Tabasco to taste

Preheat the oven to 350°.

Mix all together. Pour in a lightly buttered 8-inch square pan. Bake for 30 minutes.

Serves eight.

Green-bean Casserole

Like stuffed eggs and pimiento cheese, a green-bean casserole invariably graces the table of the Delta's bereaved. It's also part of the casserole comeback—because we've been deprived of fat, salt, and sugar too long.

Ingredients

> 4 cans (14 ½-ounce) Blue Lake green
> beans, whole
> 1 (14-ounce) can of Sweet Sue chicken
> broth
> ¼ cup bacon grease
> 1 stick unsalted butter, plus some
> for topping
> 1 ¼ cups chopped onion
> 2 cups sliced fresh mushrooms
> ¼ cup flour
> 1 cup milk
> 1 cup cream
> 1 teaspoon salt, or to taste
> 1 teaspoon white pepper
> ½ teaspoon Tabasco
> 1 teaspoon soy sauce
> 1 ¼ cups grated Swiss cheese
> 1 cup slivered almonds

Preheat the oven to 350°.

Drain the beans and cook them in the chicken broth and bacon grease, covered, for 30 minutes. Drain, reserving the cooking liquid.

Meanwhile, sauté the onions and mushrooms in butter for three to four minutes. Add, while stirring, flour, milk, and cream. Then add salt, pepper, Tabasco, and soy sauce. Finally, add the Swiss cheese and green beans to the sauce. Transfer to a 3-quart casserole, top it with the almonds, and dot with butter. Bake for 30 to 45 minutes, or until brown and bubbly.

Other toppings include the traditional can of French-fried onions, buttered bread crumbs, or a combination of both.

You can omit making the white sauce with flour, milk, and cream and simply substitute a can of cream of mushroom soup.

Serves eight.

Lemon Rice

This is a great dish to take to a funeral. It can be frozen, and it's not a goofed-up something—you can tell immediately what it is, no guesswork. It's a pleasant change from the baked rice casserole.

If you have your own chicken stock, made from scratch, you will be assured of an especially delicious dish. Canned chicken stock can be used, but your final product is just not as rich and flavorsome.

Ingredients
2 ½ cups chicken stock
1 clove garlic, minced
½ teaspoon salt
1 teaspoon white pepper
1 cup rice
1 ½ tablespoons finely grated lemon zest
1 tablespoon dried dill or 2 tablespoons fresh dill
2 tablespoons unsalted butter

Bring the chicken stock, garlic, salt, and pepper to a boil. Add the rice and cook for about 20 minutes, or until all the liquid is absorbed. Gently incorporate the lemon zest. Allow the rice to stand, covered, for a few minutes.

Stir in the dill and butter. Check the seasoning. This can be served immediately or frozen for later use.

Serves eight.

Parmesan Squash Casserole

Casseroles get better as they sit, more so after having been frozen. You can't believe it's the truth, but it is. It's too bad casseroles have such a bad name. We understand that outsiders consider them tacky, but they are the essence of funeral food in the South. I'd be hard-pressed to find one person who disagrees or passes on the buffet. When else do you get this wonderful goo?

Ingredients

12 yellow squash, cooked in salted water
   until tender
1 bunch green onions, sliced
1 clove garlic, minced
⅛ cup bacon grease
2 teaspoons Worcestershire sauce (Lea & Perrins)
2 teaspoons salt
2 teaspoons white pepper
¼ teaspoon basil
½ cup cream
2 eggs, well beaten
½ cup grated Parmesan cheese
½ cup grated Swiss cheese
cracker crumbs
butter

Preheat the oven to 350°.

Drain and mash the squash. Sauté the onions and garlic in bacon grease for 3 to 4 minutes. Add the squash, Worcestershire, salt, pepper, basil, and cream. Stir over low heat until blended.

Remove from heat. Fold in the eggs and cheeses. Pour into a buttered 3-quart casserole. Top with cracker crumbs and dot with butter.

Bake for 45 minutes, or until bubbly.

Serves eight.

Thrifty Squash Casserole

When I last "fixed" this squash (and a fix it was, since I boiled the hell out of it), I found that the frozen squash tasted better! Maybe it was the Rotel tomatoes. At any rate, the squash here in Garden City cost me twelve dollars . . . that's a dollar a piece! One of the few times in my life that the less expensive version was better.

Ingredients
  1 medium yellow onion,
    chopped
  ½ cup green pepper, chopped
  2 tablespoons butter
  2 (16-ounce) packages frozen squash
  1 cup grated sharp yellow cheese
  1 teaspoon salt
  ½ teaspoon black pepper
  1 (10-ounce) can Rotel tomatoes,
    drained
  ½ cup crumbled Ritz crackers mixed
    with ½ cup grated Parmesan cheese

Preheat the oven to 350°.

Sauté the onion and green pepper in butter for 3 or 4 minutes. Add the squash and cook until tender. Drain the squash mixture and add the yellow cheese, salt, and pepper. Fold in the tomatoes.

Place in a 2-quart buttered casserole and bake for 20 minutes.

Remove from oven and top with crackers and Parmesan cheese. Dot with butter. Bake another 20 minutes or until brown and bubbly.

Serves eight.

Healing Cheese Grits, Gouda

Few things bring more comfort than a big pot of bubbly cheese grits. In addition to the recipe for Leland Gruyere Grits, this grits recipe heals the Southern soul.

Ingredients
    1 quart homemade chicken stock
    2 quarts heavy cream
    1 pound stone-ground grits
    1 stick butter
    1 pound Gouda, diced

Bring the stock and cream to a boil. Add the grits and stir for 5 minutes, then add the butter and cook over low heat for about 30 minutes, or until smooth. Add the Gouda and stir until melted.

Serves ten.

Corn Loaf

This recipe *does* use fresh ingredients . . . but it's still comforting. Of course, it's not appropriate to serve corn on the cob, but this corn dish is perfect for a funeral. One of our non-cooking friends makes this, but only when somebody has died.

Ingredients

2 cups fresh corn kernels
1 cup chopped yellow onion
3 minced green onions
1 cup chopped green pepper
1 cup chopped tomato
2 teaspoons salt
1/4 teaspoon cayenne pepper
1 cup yellow cornmeal
1 cup grated extra-sharp cheese
2 eggs, beaten
1/2 cup evaporated milk
1/4 cup sour cream
1/4 cup water

Preheat the oven to 375°.

Combine corn, onions, green pepper, tomato, salt, cayenne, cornmeal, and cheese. Allow this to rest for 30 minutes.

Mix well-beaten eggs with evaporated milk, sour cream, and water. Be sure eggs are well incorporated into the mixture, and then mix with the vegetables. Bake in a buttered 4 ½ × 8 ½-inch loaf pan for 1 hour. Let this sit for a few minutes before slicing.

Serves six.

Viking Baked Tomatoes

This is a recipe that comes from the Viking Cooking School. Yes, Viking is in Greenwood, and Greenville historically has competed with it for the title of Queen City of the Delta. This recipe is so perfect, though, that it had to be here. It uses the same ingredients as stewed tomatoes, but looks better and can be served more appropriately at a funeral buffet.

Ingredients

3 (1-pound) cans whole tomatoes,
    drained well
zest of one lemon
2 cloves minced garlic
½ cup chopped parsley
2 cups fresh bread crumbs,
    whole wheat preferred
⅓ cup light brown sugar
⅓ cup unsalted butter, melted
salt
freshly ground pepper

Preheat the oven to 350°.

Be sure tomatoes are drained well. Combine the garlic, lemon zest, and parsley. Arrange the tomatoes in a 9 x 13-inch baking dish. Combine the bread crumbs and sugar. Add melted butter and mix well. Distribute evenly over the tomatoes. Sprinkle generously with salt and pepper. Bake for 25 minutes, or until hot and bubbling.

Serves eight.

Finger Sandwiches

Why finger sandwiches? Because you can comfortably grab a tiny sandwich and receive your guests graciously while partaking of sustenance. Not only is there an endless variety of spreads, finger sandwiches are an attractive way to make good use of the inevitable platter of slick meat from the super-market. (See "The Eternal Slick Ham Platter," page 90.) Many swear by bunny bread . . . crusts removed, of course. Thin white bread for the deviled ham and thin wheat bread for the artichoke spread are nice. Homemade bread, of course, is sublime. Whatever bread you use, the crusts *must* be removed. Or we'll haunt you. . . .

Every sandwich, finger or otherwise, is a lot better with a spread of homemade mayonnaise. Good cooks believe in a spread of butter followed by a spread of mayonnaise. With this combo, you can almost leave out the filling!

Artichoke Spread

Ingredients

2 cans artichoke hearts, drained and chopped
1 package (1-ounce) Hidden Valley creamy
   Italian dressing
¼ cup mayonnaise, homemade

Mix ingredients and season to taste. Spread on Earth-grain's thin-sliced wheat bread. Try adding a thin slice of avocado to this sandwich.

Makes fifteen finger sandwiches.

Deviled Ham and Cheese Spread

Ingredients

1 (8-ounce) package cream cheese
8 to 12 ounces pimiento cheese
1 can (4 ¼-ounces) deviled ham

Cream all ingredients together. Spread on homemade white bread with a little mayonnaise. A little piece of butter lettuce added to each sandwich is a nice touch.

Makes about three cups.

The Delta Funeral Hit Parade

Banned at St. James', Canned at the Funeral Home
  Amazing Grace
  How Great Thou Art
  Sweet Beulah Land

For the Well-Bred Dead Person
  For All the Saints
  Oh, God Our Help in Ages Past
  Lift High the Cross
  The King of Love My Shepherd Is
  A Mighty Fortress Is Our God

*All-Time Top Funeral Hit (Guaranteed to
produce tears . . . of a refined nature)*
  Abide with Me

Being Dead Doesn't Mean You Have Good Taste
  On Eagle's Wings
  In the Garden
  Beautiful Isle of Somewhere

Ne-vuh Again!
  The Battle Hymn of the Republic

One of our most revered grand dames went out to "The Battle Hymn of the Republic." It was somehow *her*. We gloried in her eccentricity, and we loved her for her daring choice. *But it had better not happen again.* "The Battle Hymn of the Republic" is most assuredly not an approved Southern funeral hymn. Miss Julia Ward Howe wrote it in 1862; at the time, you may recall, the Delta belonged to another governmental entity. Let bygones be bygones, but we don't want to hear this hymn again. Not at a funeral, anyway.

Southerners rarely get much past the age of thirty before they start working on their funerals. We are particularly concerned about the music. It was ever thus. During a yellow fever epidemic, a young doctor contracted the fatal fever. His first worry: What to sing at his funeral. He chose an old Victorian favorite, "Beautiful Isle of Somewhere," and extracted from his wife a deathbed promise that she would sing it for him.

The funeral, needless to say, was held at home. She was dying of yellow fever herself by then, but undaunted. At the appointed moment, the doors of the double parlor were rolled ponderously open to reveal the moribund woman, bravely propped up in a bed. And, of course, she was singing "Beautiful Isle of Somewhere." There was such a river of tears you would have thought that the levee had broken. She was dead within the week. Everybody felt certain that she had joined her beloved spouse. "Somewhere the sun is shining/ Somewhere the song-birds sing."

Next to the aspic, it is the hymns that make or break the Southern funeral. One prominent category—Banned at St. James', Canned at the Funeral Home—comprises the hymns that are most often requested by families that choose to hold the service at the funeral home rather than at their own homes or at the cemetery but which would never—and we mean *never*—be heard at St. James'. Unfortunately, the funeral home relies on piped-in recordings. The big three are: "Amazing Grace," "How Great Thou Art" (very great, but a very tacky song) and "Sweet Beulah Land." All are guaranteed to give the tear ducts a major workout.

"Sweet Beulah Land," written by a Methodist lay-man at a campground meeting, is rarely heard outside of the Deep South, and is the musical equivalent of Methodist cooking. Like the pineapple casserole, "Sweet Beulah Land" is a little hokey, but it grows on you: "I'm kind of homesick for that country/To which I've never been before."

"Sweet Beulah Land" has a robust melody—so robust, in fact, that, were it sung at St. James, the corpse would bump its head by sitting bolt upright in the casket. God's Frozen People prefer dirges. "Oh, God, Our Help in Ages

Past" is a favorite, and not just for Episcopalians—it's sometimes called The Calvinist National Anthem because Presbyterians—another fun group—love it too. Nice tune, can't dance to it, but it manages to be both stately and wistful, and it has decent tear-producing capability (Yes, Virginia, Episcopalians and Presbyterians do cry real tears): "Time, like an ever-rolling stream, bears all its sons away; /They fly forgotten, as a dream /Dies at the opening day." It just doesn't get much better than that.

"For All the Saints" and "Lift High the Cross," more recently in vogue, have bolder melodies. "For All the Saints" is also rather flattering to the deceased, though it's actually about saints of the official variety. The organ peal at the beginning is ideal for getting the show on the road. It sends the mourners out of the church and into the cemetery across the street. "The King of Love My Shepherd Is" is such a lilting, sweet hymn that it will almost certainly bring a gentle tear to the cheek of most mourners.

For quiet tears, though, nothing beats "Abide with Me," a favorite among the older Christian hymns. Even many non-churchgoers know the words (". . . fast falls the eventide; The darkness deepens. . . ."). Its composer was Henry Francis Lyte, an Anglican minister, who was—naturally—dying. He wrote it for his last sermon, preached in Devonshire, England. Though we associate this hymn with funerals, it was sung at the weddings of King George VI and Queen Elizabeth II. This royal pedigree should do wonders to revive its flagging popularity among Delta snobs.

"On Eagle's Wings" was born in the Catholic Church, but it has spread like kudzu. Though it was sung at the funeral of John F. Kennedy Jr., the mere thought of it can keep any ailing Deltan alive for several months. "On Eagle's Wings" is the jolly hockey sticks approach to death. It's pure kitsch; the only time it's ever worked was when it was played on a violin in the cemetery, and nobody sang its silly words. We wondered if the August heat, playing havoc with the strings, had somehow improved it. But most of us will not go out with a violin in the cemetery. Don't soar "On Eagle's Wings."

A good rule of thumb if you want to have a perfect Southern funeral: No hymns composed after 1940.

6

Suitably Boxed:
Meringue Shells,
Pecan Tassies . . . and You

After leading an exciting life in the big city—New York or New Orleans—many Delta natives return home suitably boxed. Being buried in Greenville means that they will find themselves surrounded by the same annoying relatives they left town to escape. But now, of course, it won't matter. "I can't stand half the people on our plot," said Lutie Bartlett, whose moonlight-on-the-old-plantation accent is so thick as to be unintelligible even to us. A longtime Manhattanite, Lutie is fond of announcing to a room full of perfect strangers who just don't give a hoot that she loves the South so much she would die for it. She'd rather die than live there, too. Still, to her eternal credit, she is planning to be dead here.

Throughout her long exile, the expatriate's heart is warmed by thoughts of her eventual homecoming. Nothing brings more solace to Southerners far from home than the thought of a gaping hole on the family plot reserved just for them. Lutie is no different. She has dibs on a place near her mother on the cemetery's main drag. She lives in fear that her worthless cousin Fred, who covets her spot, will try to beat her out of it by dying first. She's determined not to let this happen, whatever it takes! "When I end up planted next to Mama," she said, sounding like she's trying out for the remake of *Baby Doll*, "it'll be the first time Aunt Weezy and I ever got within ten feet of each other without her telling me to stand up straight and brush the hair out of my eyes."

Some Southerners must spend many years in exile before their accent reaches its full potential. Lutie has lived in New York two decades, and her accent is so thick we wonder if she has a Berlitz coach. She pines day and night for the sacred Southland, and is fond of bragging, "Mah grandmother had enough silver to feed Lee's army." She hints that the Wah-wuh still hangs heavy upon her. Nothing pleases her more than being invited by some unsuspecting soul to visit Grant's tomb. This affords her an opportunity to draw herself up and say, "Ah would rather die than betray mah people that way."

As a member of the Magnolia Mafia, Lutie is proud that one night, when blind drunk, she ordered her taxi to halt, then stepped out and released her dinner on a statue of General

Sherman near the Plaza Hotel. As is often the case with the homes of Delta exiles, Lutie's apartment is a shrine to Mississippi, filled with old land grants, photographs of plantations, and other ancestral mementos. Lutie has not attained the level of Gothic creepiness another belle has achieved on New York's Upper East Side. Southerners love ancestral portraits and silver more than life itself, and when they are feeling down, they like to remind themselves that, unlike Yankees, they have ancestors. But instead of just hanging an ancestral portrait above her mantel, this belle of the Southland put an ancestor on the mantel—her mother's purloined ashes. Her brother is frantically trying to reclaim Mama, but, just having Mama in New York makes Lutie's friend feel more at home. She is endeavoring to write a novel about her rapport with the maternal cinders but said this is proving tiresomely difficult because the relationship "is still evolving."

Like other Southerners who live in exile and go around acting like they believe the characters in *Gone with the Wind* are real people, Lutie has a dirty little secret: she *can* go home again. Any time she wants to. But what for? Back home, everybody is Southern, and you don't get a whole heck of a lot of mileage out of it. People in Greenville never say, "Where did you get that cute Southern accent?" Exotic tales of aristocratic inbreeding don't make a big impression on us because down here we're all our own third cousin (at least, everybody nice is).

There may be no other place on earth where a Southerner can feel as Southern as in New York City. But being dead there is another matter. For that, you want to go home. Of course, there are special logistical challenges posed by the funeral of one long absent, not the least of which is getting here. You would think cremation would simplify matters, but it doesn't. When his uncle Boatner died in New York, Henry K. Bartlett went to fetch Boaty's belongings and was entrusted with an urn containing Boaty himself. All Henry K. had to do was hang onto Boaty for two or three days. As the family was driving serenely into the cemetery, Henry K.'s mother idly inquired if the ashes were already there. "I reckon so," Henry K. said, shrugging. "I mailed them a few days ago." Boaty was still in the loving care of the United States Postal Service, but the funeral had to go on so as not to disappoint the out-of-town guests.

Willie Johnson was a photographer who rolled her own cigarettes from Bull Durham tobacco and wore a Panama or bowler hat handsomely set off with other articles of masculine attire such as pin-striped trousers or a coat and four-in-hand tie—the family insisted she'd been engaged to a nice young *man* from Inverness, Mississippi, but it "just hadn't worked out." The suitor of a relative almost didn't marry into the family because of Willie. He didn't care about the men's clothing, but she was a *lady photographer*. After Willie had had enough of amusing Greenville, she went to live in an artists' colony in New Mexico. Eventually, she ended up in an old ladies home run by nuns, and we can only assume that the good sisters got an earful of bad language, because Willie cussed—and drank—like a sailor. Nonetheless, when she died, she left behind instructions that she was to be buried in Greenville, of course.

Although Willie wouldn't have dreamed of being laid to rest anywhere but the old cemetery, her family's attachment to the cemetery was a recent phenomenon. They hailed from Kentucky and for their first six or seven decades as residents of Mississippi had insisted upon sending their dead back to the Blue Grass State. It is never easy for a Southerner to adjust to a new burial ground. Even those members of the family born in the Delta made the posthumous trek to the old burial ground in Kentucky. If somebody died in the depths of winter or at some other inopportune time, he or she was temporarily stored in a brick vault on a plantation near Lake Washington—a hub of families that had come from Kentucky at the turn of the century, a few miles from Greenville—and then disinterred when the weather got nice. It was the Wah-wuh Between the States that finally put the kibosh on this practice. The first of Willie's kin to be permanently dead in the Delta was a young bride who'd married while the hostilities were in full swing. "Times were too difficult to take her anywhere else," Willie's cousin John Erwin lamented. He added, "So she stayed put and the river got her." It is an unfortunate tendency of floods in Mississippi to play havoc with private, family cemeteries, not infrequently causing bodies to rise to the top and float off. Many of Willie's family had found themselves being carried away—but not to their old Kentucky homes. One of Willie's cousins received a frantic call from somebody regarding a dead relative who had done just that. "Colonel Matt's done got a-loose," the cousin was informed. The floating uncle was reburied in the Greenville cemetery. The last of the family to suffer the indignity of drowning while dead seems to have been a little bitty baby, whose tiny little coffin was washed up in 1927, the year of the big flood. Bubba Boone's great-uncle Buddy Boy Boone, who preceded Bubba in the family business, had to fetch the runaway coffin for reburial. Though no stranger to the clammy hand of death, Buddy Boy frankly admitted that the baby coffin "skeered me to death."

On one of the hottest days in the summer of 1950, Willie's friends and kin gathered on the family plot. Everybody was there but Willie. The assembled milled around and gossiped; the men sweated bullets and the women glowed (which is what ladies do instead of sweating) all the while trying to pretend that Willie wasn't committing the faux pas of being late to her funeral. They waited and waited. After a while, even the old ladies weren't able to enjoy themselves for fear of heat stroke. Finally, Mrs. Chowtard Theobold hove into sight in her green Oldsmobile with her driver, Julius, behind the wheel. Julius tooted the horn, and Mrs. Theobold lowered her window and leaned out the car. "Yoo-hoo! Yoo-hoo!" she trilled. "Willie missed connections in Albuquerque. Come back tomorrow."

And everybody did come back the next day. There was one of those summer rains, but Willie—and her mourners—made it this time. Everybody but Willie got drenched. "Don't you know she'd love it that we had to go to her funeral twice?" said Olivia Morgan Gilliam.

Like Willie, the Reverend Smythe Smith's mother had found the Delta constraining in her later years. She moved to California and kicked up her aged heels. But she, too, wouldn't be caught dead anywhere but Greenville. Smythe's overriding concern was making sure his mother was buried in her favorite charcoal gray suit. He knew that, alive or dead, Southern ladies want to be nicely turned out. The very idea of an open coffin visitation makes the Southern lady want every strand of hair and her makeup to be perfect. When Bubba Boone ushered Smythe up to the coffin, Smythe let out a long sigh. "Mother always loved that suit," he murmured dreamily. He peered closer. "But *that is not my mother.*"

Bubba took this personally and went stiffer than the body in the box. "I know my own mother," Smythe persisted. Bubba was fit to be tied. Being a minister, Smythe wasn't scared of dead bodies, so he reached into the coffin and pulled out a tag—it identified the strange body as belonging to a lady from Natchez, Mississippi. Rising to the occasion, Smythe quickly ordered the coffin closed, and the reception went on as if nothing were amiss. Not a soul guessed that the real Agnes Jane Smith was at that moment wearing a tacky, plumb colored polyester dress in a Natchez funeral home. The caskets had been switched in transit. It seems that the Natchez family wasn't terribly observant, and only Bubba's timely phone call saved Agnes Jane from being buried in the wrong grave. "Oh, well," Smythe said, "Mother did always want to get to the Natchez Pilgrimage."

Whether you have lived all your life in our midst or

sojourned elsewhere, you can count on Delta ladies baking for your funeral. Although tomato aspic with homemade mayonnaise is the signature dish of death, the sweets are actually more abundant and go faster than any other foods at a Southern funeral. Every Southern lady has a specialty sweet recipe for which she is famous—even those Southern ladies who ordinarily can't cook.

Flowers of Southern womanhood who wouldn't be caught dead dredging a roast or frizzling a piece of ham are inordinately vain about their divinities, toffees, or caramel cakes. We know one non-cook who used to make divinity for the church bazaar and then hover menacingly at the display to prevent anybody from choosing her sister-in-law's divinity instead. One of these non-cooks, Olivia Morgan, belatedly became aware of the Moon Pie. The Moon Pie is the South's great bargain meal, a sort of marshmallow sandwich with a chocolate, vanilla, or banana coating. The Moon Pie was developed in a bakery in Chattanooga, Tennessee, and it was traditionally washed down with an RC Cola. It soon became the quintessential redneck delicacy. Somehow this sheltered belle had never encountered the Moon Pie-mystique. It's hard to believe, but Olivia was even vaguer than most Southern ladies of the older generation, which is saying a lot. When her gaze lit upon the Moon Pie, she experienced inspiration. She stepped out of her non-cook mode to create a new dessert, built entirely around the Moon Pie. The plebian Moon Pie was doused with crème de menthe and embedded in homemade ice cream, which was frozen so hard that even Eskimos would have needed a hot plate. The concoction was certainly hard enough to break a dessert spoon. The new creation was brought into the dining room with some degree of fanfare. It was too hard to eat, even if somebody had wanted to.

Everybody else in the family knew what a Moon Pie was, and they were instantly horrified at being served one for Sunday dinner. There was dead silence. "How do you like my new dessert? I call it my Moon Surprise," Olivia Morgan sang out. She should have called it her Moon Shock.

Fortunately, most Southern cooks don't dabble in Moon Pies, and the sweets are beautiful, delicious, and abundant. "If you don't get at least one caramel cake when you die in the Delta," said Amanda Rucks, "somebody doesn't love you." Because cookies and smaller sweets can be left out all day and served with coffee, and the big, pretty, luscious cakes are always on the buffet table for lunch or dinner before or after the funeral, there are seldom any sweets left over. No self-respecting member of Delta society would rest in peace unless reasonably certain that the minute his friends and family make their final farewells—and finish gossiping with each other at the graveside—they'll return home and find enough delicious sweets to kill them then and there.

Mother's Banana Nut Bread

Banana nut bread is a lot like stuffed eggs in that it is standard at a funeral. The difference is that you can use the nut bread in many more ways, and it can even be frozen for later. You can toast and butter it for breakfast or for lunch. For lunch, Anne Call spreads a gooey mixture of cream cheese and marmalade or crystallized ginger on thin slices to make a sandwich. I like mine plain in the late afternoon. I freeze my overly ripe bananas and use them later because they are stronger in flavor. However, if you do this, you must decrease the number of bananas by one.

Ingredients
    4 cups flour
    2 teaspoons baking powder
    2 teaspoons soda
    1 cup unsalted butter
    2 cups sugar
    4 eggs
    6 ripe bananas, mashed
    2 cups chopped nuts

Preheat the oven to 325°.

Sift the flour, baking powder, and soda together. Cream together the butter and sugar. Add the eggs and mix. Add flour mixture to the butter, sugar, and egg mixture. Fold in the mashed bananas.

Lightly flour the nuts and fold them into the banana mixture.

Bake for 1 hour in a buttered loaf pan (4 ½ x 8 ½-inches). Glaze if desired.

Glaze

  2 cups powdered sugar
  2 tablespoons butter, softened
  4 to 6 tablespoons milk

In a small bowl, blend the above ingredients until smooth. Remove the bread from the pan and spoon the glaze over it.

Makes one loaf.

Southern Sideboard's Rich Bourbon Dessert

There is a tacko recipe called Death by Chocolate that's been around for years. This is an upscale—but not that upscale—version of Death by Chocolate. Not to be confused with Death by Chicken (see p. 147).

(see p. 147)

Ingredients
    5 dozen individually wrapped Amaretti macaroons
    1 cup good bourbon
    2 cups unsalted butter, softened
    2 cups sugar
    1 dozen eggs, separated
    4 (1-ounce) squares unsweetened chocolate, melted
    1 ½ teaspoons vanilla
    1 cup chopped pecans
    2 dozen lady fingers
    2 cups whipping cream, whipped
    confectioners' sugar

Soak the macaroons in the bourbon. Cream the butter and sugar until light. Beat the egg yolks until light, and blend in to the sugar/butter mixture. Fold the chocolate into the mixture. Add the vanilla and pecans, mixing gently. Whip the egg whites until stiff, and fold into the chocolate mixture.

Line a 10-inch springform pan, bottom and sides, with lady fingers. Pour a layer of the chocolate mixture into the springform pan, and then add a layer of bourbon-soaked macaroons, alternating layers and ending with the chocolate mixture. Cover the pan and chill overnight.

When ready to serve, remove the sides of the pan. Nap with whipped cream that has been flavored with confectioners' sugar and a bit of bourbon to taste.

Serves eighteen.

Sad Cake

I don't know if this cake is called Sad Cake because the poor thing is made with Bisquick or because you see it at funerals. Sad Cake can be cut in squares and served from early morning to late afternoon with coffee and tea. Actually, it does not even resemble a cake!

Ingredients
    1 ½ cups Bisquick
    1 (1-pound) box light brown sugar
    4 eggs, lightly beaten
    ⅓ cup oil
    1 cup shredded coconut
    1 cup pecan pieces, not too small

Preheat the oven to 350°.

Mix together the Bisquick and sugar, and make a well in the center. Pour the eggs, oil, coconut and pecans into this indentation, and stir until well mixed. Generously butter a 9 × 13-inch pan. Pour the mixture evenly into the pan. Bake for no longer than 45 minutes.

Makes two dozen lady-like squares.

Julia Morgan Hall Hays's Toffee

There must be a reason toffee sounds like toff. Crumbled up over coffee ice cream with a dash of crème de cacao, it is one of life's great indulgences. Alas, this rendition of toffee would melt at a funeral while everybody was busy gossiping. Just plain though, toffee served with coffee or on the dessert tray couldn't be more appropriate.

Ingredients
- 1 pound butter
- 1 pound sugar (2 ½ cups)
- 1 pound chopped pecans
- 1 giant Hershey's bar

Cook the butter and sugar together over medium heat, stirring often, until it is the color of the pecans. Add the pecans and spread this mixture on a buttered cookie sheet. Put in the icebox to harden. Melt half the Hershey's bar and spread it on top of the hard toffee. Sprinkle the top with chopped pecans and put it back in the icebox to harden. Flip the toffee over and spread the other side with the rest of the Hershey's and pecans. Harden again and break or cut the toffee into pieces.

Makes about two to three pounds.

Meringue Shells

Everybody in Greenville of a certain age remembers going on Saturday afternoons to pick up the meringue shells for Sunday lunch at the old Brown's Bakery. Filled with peppermint ice cream or some other delicious and color-appropriate concoction, they made a memorable finale for the roast beef (which in those days was often woefully overcooked in the South) and creamed peas in pastry shells, two Sunday lunch favorites. Meringue shells are a nice offering for a funeral, either for dessert or on the buffet.

This recipe comes from Jane Hovas, a good friend and stalwart of Presbyterian funeral cooking. It's a known fact that some of her friends near death have requested her meringues. Of course, Jane's friends hoped they'd arrive *before* the funeral. Still, they do keep well.

Ingredients
    3 large eggs, whites only
    1 cup sugar
    $\frac{1}{2}$ teaspoon white vinegar
    1 teaspoon vanilla

Preheat the oven to 225°.

Beat the egg whites until a peak will hold. Add the sugar, a little at a time, beating all the while. After all the sugar has been added, the whites are stiff, and there is no grainy texture, add the vinegar and vanilla, and beat until incorporated . . . not too long.

Drop small teaspoons of the meringue onto buttered baking sheets. With the back of the spoon, make an indention in each mound . . . as deep as possible without piercing the bottom.

Bake on the lower shelf of your oven for 45 minutes, or until lightly browned. Do not overbake. Watch carefully the last few minutes. Gently remove the meringues and cool completely. These can be stored in an airtight tin or frozen.

Makes about five dozen shells.

Lime Curd for Meringue Shells

Ingredients

- 1 tablespoon grated lime zest
- ⅔ cup lime juice (key lime, bottled)
- 2 cups sugar
- 2 sticks unsalted butter, sliced
- 4 eggs, lightly beaten

In the top of a double boiler, combine the zest, juice, sugar, and butter. Cook over medium heat until the butter melts, stirring continuously. Incorporate a small amount of it into the eggs. Add the egg mixture to the remaining lime mixture in the top of the double boiler. Continue stirring and cooking until the mixture thickens, about 15 minutes.

Remove from heat and cool before refrigerating. This will keep in the refrigerator for two weeks.

Makes enough for two dozen tartlets.

Chocolate Chess Pie

Chess pie is a classic Southern sweet, and the good news is that you don't have to ask the specialty grocer to order some chesses. There's no such thing. A chess pie is simply a pie made from sugar, butter, egg yolks, and a smidgen of flour.

Nobody knows why it is called a chess pie. The name may come from an Old English tradition of calling various sweets with a curdlike texture cheesecakes. Or it could be derived from the name of a piece of furniture, the pie chest. Because of its high sugar content, a chess pie stayed fresh in an unrefrigerated pie ches' longer than other pies. The most charming explanation is that a housewife, when asked the name of the delicious dessert she was serving, replied, "Jes' pie."

Ingredients

2 cups sugar
4 ½ teaspoons cocoa
3 tablespoons flour
pinch salt
1 ½ sticks margarine, melted
3 eggs
1 small (5-ounce) can Pet milk
2 tablespoons regular, full-leaded milk
2 teaspoons vanilla
1 unbaked pie shell, or see recipe that
    follows for a delicious crust

Preheat the oven to 325°.

Mix the sugar, cocoa, flour, and salt. Add the remaining ingredients. Mix well. Pour the mixture into the pie shell. Bake for 45 minutes, or until set.

Serves eight

A Delicious Pie Crust

A homemade pie crust beats a store-bought one any day of the week. This one can make the chess pie even better.

Ingredients
1 tablespoon all-purpose flour
2 cups chopped pecans
$\frac{1}{4}$ cup sugar
$\frac{1}{4}$ cup margarine, softened

Combine all ingredients and press into a 9-inch pie pan.

Pecan Tassies

In the movie *Steel Magnolias*, Clairee walks into the beauty shop with a plate of her "annual pecan tassies." Southerners love pecan tassies. They're miniature tarts with a pecan filling.

Ingredients
    1 (3-ounce) package cream
        cheese
    1 stick unsalted butter,
        softened
    1 ¼ cups flour

Filling
    ½ cup chopped pecans
    1 beaten egg
    1 tablespoon melted butter
    ½ to ¾ teaspoon vanilla

Mix the cream cheese, butter, and flour until blended. I use a food processor. Refrigerate for at least an hour. Press a small amount of dough into a mini muffin tin, making about 30 shells.

Mix together the pecans, egg, melted butter, and vanilla. Using a demitasse spoon, fill each unbaked shell halfway with this mixture. Bake at 325°no longer than 20 minutes.

Makes thirty miniature tarts.

NOTE: These can be frozen.

Bland's Fake Pineapple Upside-down Cake

A food snob, Bland Shackelford Currie calls this fake because she uses a mix to make the cake. Don't let her intimidate you about the maraschino cherries, which enhance the cake. This is Bland's recipe, in her own words.

Ingredients

1 box Uncle Dunkie's butter-flavored
   yellow cake mix
¾ box light brown sugar
1 stick butter
1 small can sliced pineapple (reserve liquid)
maraschino cherries (for tacky people), drained
vanilla

Melt the butter and brown sugar in a 9-inch black-iron skillet. Remove from heat and add the pineapple and optional tacky cherries in a decorative fashion.

Follow the directions on the box of Uncle Dunkie's butter-flavored yellow cake mix, using the reserved pineapple juice instead of water. Add an extra egg and some vanilla. Pour the mixture on top of pineapple mixture and bake according to the box temperature. Turn out onto a lovely cake plate with a doily and serve.

Serves twelve.

Can't-Die-Without-It Caramel Cake

The Delta abounds with wonderful recipes for caramel cake. This particular one is a First Methodist favorite created by the late Gertrude Sorrells.

Ingredients
    1 box Duncan Hines butter cake mix
    4 eggs
    1 stick butter
    ⅔ cup water

Caramel Icing
    3 cups sugar
    1 cup Pet milk
    ¼ teaspoon salt
    1 teaspoon vanilla
    1 stick butter

Follow package instructions for cake. Allow to cool.

In the top of a double boiler, mix 2 ½ cups of the sugar with the Pet milk. Add salt. Boil for 3 minutes, stirring the entire time. Remove from heat.

Pour ½ cup sugar into a black-iron skillet and caramelize it. To carmelize is to melt the sugar over medium heat—

stirring constantly until the syrup turns a golden brown. This can burn, so be careful.

Pour the milk mixture into the skillet, mix well, and transfer it back into the double boiler. Add butter and vanilla. Put the top of the double boiler in a cold water bath and stir the mixture until cold and thick. Spread on the cake.

Serves twelve.

Mrs. Call's Orange Cake

Simple but delicious. At this writing, Anne Call is 92, and this recipe has been around about that long.

Ingredients
   1 cup butter
   1 cup sugar
   3 eggs, separated
   1 cup dairy sour cream
   grated rind of 1 orange
   1 ¾ cup all-purpose flour
   1 teaspoon baking powder
   1 teaspoon baking soda

Cream the butter and sugar. Add the egg yolks, sour cream, and orange rind. Beat until light and fluffy. Sift together the flour, baking powder, and baking soda. Stir into the first mixture.

Beat the egg whites until stiff, but NOT dry. Fold into the mixture. Turn the batter into an oiled and floured (10-cup) bundt pan. Allow to sit ten minutes.

Bake in a preheated 325° oven for 1 hour. Remove the pan from the oven and let it stand for 10 minutes.

Loosen the cake carefully around the edges and turn it out onto a plate with a rim. Immediately pour hot orange syrup over the top of the cake. Slice thinly.

Orange Syrup
    juice of 2 oranges
    juice of 1 lemon
    ¾ cup sugar
    dash salt

Combine these ingredients and boil 3 to 4 minutes. Immediately pour over cake.

Serves fifteen.

Southern Funeral Flowers

Don'ts

carnations (with or without glitter)

gladiolus

all eternal (artificial) flowers

leatherleaf ferns (the standard florist filler—beware)

a "designer arrangement" that turns out to be a floral
   clock with the hands stopped at the time of death

Do's

greenery from your very own plantation

a covering for the coffin woven from yardlike flowers

all-white yardlike flowers

the traditional bouquet of roses, all the same color
   (white or a delicate pink)

a beautiful white standing spray in the shape of a cross
   using Casablanca lilies or the like—the delicate
   scent will waft over the cemetery. Of course, this
   might not be appreciated in less traditional parts
   of the country, but the fragrance is terrific.

When our dear Augusta Jones died, her father went to the florist and sat on a stool studying roses, or pictures of roses, until he found the perfect shade of pink to blanket her coffin. "This is too hot," he would say, or "This is too faded." He settled on a delicate pink with the merest hint of sauciness. It was somehow just right for Augusta, a saucy Southern lady. The roses provided a nice contrast to the colors of the dry hedges of the cemetery in August. (Why do we always seem to be dying when it's hotter than Hades or so cold the shovels practically break?) All of Augusta's friends, unprompted, casually took a rose as the crowd milled around after the graveside service. Most of them still have their rose, a memento, dried and put away in a safe place, or hanging on a dressing table mirror. (Always hang flowers upside down to dry, and do not leave them in a plastic bag, as they will disintegrate rather than dry.)

Augusta's friends, moved by the premature loss of an old friend, just happened to think of taking a rose. It was not planned. They would have died of embarrassment before they'd have trooped solemnly by the coffin, in a formal line, plucking their roses. That would have smacked of a recent innovation that has "funeral director" written all over it—like the practice of having the pall bearers file past the coffin, placing their boutonnières on it. Funerals are emotional enough to begin with—

why do something that is contrived to tug at the heart? The heart doesn't need any extra tugging. It's always a good idea to talk to the funeral director in advance (and in detail), otherwise you might end up with the parade of the boutonnières (or worse).

Southern ladies love flowers almost as much as they love tomato aspic. Taste and care, not the amount of money you spend, is what matters most. A blanket of roses from the florist to cover the coffin is beautiful, but yard flowers can be just as pleasant. Remember the lady we told you about who was surreptitiously trying to switch cards on the standing spray she'd sent? She'd probably spent a small fortune on the nightmare in carnations that stood a few feet from the coffin. Although carnations, particularly the tiny ones, can be quite lovely, they tend to bring out the worst in a florist. Our worst fear (and one that is all too often realized) is that they will arrive in an unnatural hue, or with glitter! When ordering flowers, garden-club ladies are careful to specify: NO carnations or gladiolus. There's no other way to say it: Glads are just plain tacky. They may resemble the more ladylike members of the lily family, but somehow they just aren't as nice.

When the FTD triangles arrive, some caring soul takes them apart and rearranges the flowers in more natural forms, and in more appealing containers. When sending flowers to a funeral in another town, it's best to use a recommended local florist. If you don't know a florist, here are some damage-control tips: Since the person who sends the flowers rarely has the pleasure of seeing what the florist has done, it is a good idea to ask for specific flowers; if the budget is constrained, go for quality over quantity; the line of least resistance is to request one type of flower—all pink roses or all red roses (mixing is tricky. So are ribbons—which are cheap—and are all too often used as a sort of Hamburger Helper for flowers—which are not so cheap. You can control this to a degree by being specific about what you want).

Of course, the ideal is flowers from the yard. One woman, whose childhood friend had been killed in an accident, made a gorgeous covering for the coffin completely from flowers from her own yard. She is a gifted gardener and flower arranger. For those who aren't, it's a good idea to take your flowers to a florist: You don't want the floral blanket on a coffin to be deader than the person inside. (The rules on flowers for the coffin vary. Some churches do not allow flowers on the coffin during the service, when the casket is customarily covered by a pall, a cloth belonging to the church. The same pall is used for everybody who is buried from that church—as a symbol of our equality in death. The pall is placed on the coffin when it enters the church and removed as it leaves—one minister we know says the rule with the pall is door-to-door. The flowers can be returned to the coffin at the door of the church and are there for the cemetery.)

Sometimes, of course, fresh flowers aren't feasible. If Florence Metcalfe could have picked her exit date, we feel certain that it would have been when the camellias were in bloom. But we can't arrange these things, can we? She died in the depths of winter. The solution: cut greenery from her beloved Newstead Plantation, where she had spent her entire life. The greens were taken to Miz Hazel at the florist, who wove them into a covering for the coffin. The only flowers at the funeral, a graveside service in the family cemetery, were a basket of white tulips at the entrance to the burial ground. We feel certain she would have been pleased, even without the camellias.

7

The Restorative Cocktail

 A wedding takes six months to plan and put on, but a funeral—which is almost as big a deal in the Delta—must be done in two or three days, tops, even though many of the same logistical challenges apply. We devote ourselves to the ritual of the church, the food, and the visiting with the same intensity as for a wedding, only speeded up—and funerals are often bigger than weddings. "Where but the Delta will you find five hundred people at a funeral that's not the president of the United States or Kay Graham?" the rector of St. James' asked after the funeral of a particularly beloved member of our small community.

As with a wedding, friends and family come from all over. If you're in the Memphis airport waiting to risk life and limb on the commuter plane to Greenville, and you hear somebody who vaguely looks like they could be a third cousin once removed of somebody you know insisting, "But I *have* to get there by ten in the morning," you're likely to offer a handshake and say, "I bet you are going to the such-and-such funeral."

Some Delta families think of their guest bedroom as the death chamber because it is in peak demand for funerals. People come from all around to pay their respects, but also because they hate to miss a good funeral. When Mr. Lamar Jones died and Augusta couldn't come up from New Orleans, we felt sorrier for Augusta than for Mr. Lamar. "It was just the kind of Old Greenville funeral Gussie loves," Roberta Shaw said and sighed wistfully.

One of the fastest-turnaround funerals was, in fact, the funeral of Mrs. Robert Shaw, Roberta's mother, a good example of how our community can pull together when the chips are down. One night, when Roberta was home from college, she went to the Orbit Lounge and invited the band and all the patrons out to Runnymede Plantation, where they made enough noise to wake the dead (and would have if Runnymede had been about half a mile closer to the cemetery). It was quite a party, and it would have been talked about even if Mrs. Shaw hadn't died the next morning. Rest assured, she did not die because every known hoodlum in the Delta was in her back-yard shooting dice and hollering, "Eight skate and donate."

She had gone to Jackson for a routine checkup and there were unexpected complications. News of the loss hit like a bombshell, and Roberta's friends immediately disregarded their throbbing hangovers and hastened to Runnymede to eradicate the incriminating evidence of the previous evening's impromptu fete. This is what we mean by community spirit. Because that's the kind of pull-together town we are, the cigarette butts, empty beer bottles, and the makeshift bleacher (assembled for partygoers to listen to the band) had all been hauled off by the time the guests began arriving to pay their respects. Even the inert body of Fishy Freddie Ferguson—the only boy at E. E. Bass Junior High old enough to have a draft-board problem, who had passed out in Mrs. Shaw's bed of prize-winning camellias after some serious, non-underage imbibing—had been removed from the premises.

Some people may hire wedding consultants, but for the funeral we rely on tradition—and input from veterans of Delta funerals past. What makes the Delta funeral different from others is the large number of friends who get into the act. When somebody especially popular dies, we worry about creating a three-car pile-up going to the house. It is not just the immediate family that is concerned with making the funeral come off perfectly. "I couldn't listen to the sermon Sunday because I was thinking about getting home to make my aspic to take to the family on Monday," Dabney Archer has been overheard to say. As one of the Delta's premiere aspic makers, Dabney frequently has recourse to the 1-800 number for Aspic World (as the people in the Delta refer to Knox gelatin company) to chat about doubling or tripling the recipe. "I'd hate to show up with aspic that looked like it was made by B. F. Goodrich," she explained. She has never brought anything that was less than perfect, though I understand the Aspic World people had to talk her down once when the aspic wouldn't gel properly.

We still have calling cards in the Delta, and, though we no longer leave them in a silver salver (after making a hasty retreat from the house of somebody we didn't really want to visit anyway), we do have many uses for them, including attaching them to the funeral food offering. We write what we brought on the other side. This is not because we insist upon being thanked but because we know we will be, and we want to make it as easy as possible for the family member in charge of notes to do so without being embarrassed by not having the foggiest what we brought.

While a wedding reception is likely to have a caterer, funeral food comes from just about everybody you've ever known. Even though the bereaved sometimes get so much food that they have to ask neighbors to let them borrow freezer space, everybody is always obsessed with the notion that there won't be enough and the out-of-town guests will go away hungry. This is a major topic of conversation. We say things like, "Sally Stephens is out of town, so who's going to bring stuffed eggs?" We don't want another death brought on by starvation. This may be relevant with regard to our Campbell's-cream-of-mushroom-soup fixation. "Why would you want to ruin perfectly good, fresh vegetables by drenching them in Campbell's cream of mushroom soup?" a naïve matron once asked. Silly woman. "As an extender," came the reply. In addition to feeding the masses, Campbell's is regarded by many in the Delta as the ultimate in taste enhancement. (See "There is a Balm in Campbell's Soup," pp. 141–174)

The people who get the biggest bang out of funeral-going may surprise you: old ladies. You'd think they might be inspired to reflect fearfully on their own mortality. But this is not the case. They live for funerals. "I'd never see anybody if I didn't go to funerals," old Mrs. Eustis chirped. "Did you have a good time?" Olivia Morgan's daughter always asked when her mother returned from a funeral with a new spring in her step. "Oh, you don't enjoy funerals," she always replied—with a sly glint in her eye. She was highly gratified to have been present for one of the great moments in local funeral-going: when Mr. Hicks died, his mistress of fifty years, whom he'd kept in an apartment in Leland, showed up at the funeral home and *went down the receiving line.*

Delta funerals don't end the minute the last "amen" is uttered. We stand around in the cemetery visiting so long that somebody once threatened to put up a margarita stand. One thing we will say: If weddings bring out the worst in people, funerals bring out the best. We go out of our way to be nice to each other. Some of our more fragile old ladies are forced to wait in the car while the burial rite takes place, and you see people who ordinarily wouldn't give you the time of day sprinting over to make sure they say something nice to them.

In the past, the funeral was followed by an official period of mourning. Delta widows adopted Queen Victoria as their role model. Like Queen Victoria after the death of Prince Albert, they spent the remainder of their days grieving their loss, conspicuously decked out in their widow's weeds. Their wardrobes consisted entirely of black dresses, black hats, and black gloves. "Poor little thing. She never wore colors again," has been the doleful epitaph of more than one Delta widow. Although the formal rules of mourning allowed for a gradual return to normal colors, perpetual mourning was the mark of the really serious widow.

Although the Delta widow of today is likely to be wearing fire engine red and engaged to be remarried (to a man whose availability she discovered by perusing the obituaries) at just about the time the dowager of a previous generation was in the process of transitioning from jet black into dark cottons, Delta people are still relatively old-fashioned about the customs surrounding death. We don't go to big parties after a death in the family, and surviving family members are expected to behave with a degree of decorum.

While the rules of mourning are now much more relaxed, you can still run up against them. Ella Bartlett did just this when her annoying sister-in-law Polly died at the most inconvenient time of the year: a week before the Queen of Hearts Ball. This was the pièce de résistance of the local social season. Ella had moved to town and clawed her way into the garden club. But her greatest achievement was that she got to hang a banner above her front door (or did she call it a hatchment?) after her grandson had been chosen to be a page at the Queen of Hearts Ball. She could not have been more puffed up if it had been sent straight from Buckingham Palace. But then Polly selfishly died. Even in an age when the rules of mourning are perhaps too relaxed, you can't hang a banner over your hatchment during a family funeral. Ella attempted bribery, offering free airline tickets to nieces and nephews willing to move up the date of the funeral. When this didn't work, she hung her banner an hour after Polly was in the ground. Even the niece whom she'd flown in first class talked bad about her.

The funeral is always a time of stress, and everybody realizes that immediately afterward you need two things: friends and alcohol. It would be frowned upon if you went to a black-tie ball or were spotted dancing your feet off at the Four Oaks Supper Club. But a friend is certainly entitled to entertain you for a restorative cocktail. Some families return from the funeral and begin the restorative cocktail party then, finishing off the Ritz-cracker-encrusted pineapple casserole on the spot. Others prefer their restorative cocktail a bit later, at a close friend's house.

One of the other reasons for the restorative cocktail is that out-of-town guests will want to see people before they go home again. Whether as immediate relief after the funeral or solace in the following days or weeks, the restorative cocktail heralds the return to normal life. You may make use of all the funeral leftovers, but you also begin to return to normal foods. Hello pickled shrimp, goodbye pineapple casserole. Getting slightly pickled yourself is not frowned upon. It is also a good time to reminisce about the person who has died and to celebrate life.

Bland's Crabmeat

There is nothing bland about this mouth-watering crabmeat dish, except the name of its mastermind, Bland Shackelford Currie, and she's the least bland person in the Ark-La-Miss, a true Vindaloo of the spirit. A word about capers (This is very important): Bland begs that we remind you not to use those big chunky ones, but to use instead "nice lady" capers, the smaller, more delicate ones. "Nice lady" is an adjective in the Delta. Some things are nice lady and some things aren't nice lady. Nice lady is cutting the crusts off the bread before making sandwiches, using only breasts to make chicken salad, and remembering to say "little ships go out to sea" when children are eating soup incorrectly. This is a nice lady way to correct children without hurting their feelings or raising your voice (not nice lady). A really nice lady might consider little plates and napkins because a tiny plate of goodies is more conducive to reminiscing than hovering around the table.

Ingredients
    1 pound fresh jumbo lump crabmeat
    Juice of 1 lemon
    ½ cup homemade mayonnaise
    1 (3 ¼-ounce) jar capers, drained and rinsed

Squeeze the lemon over the crabmeat (be sure all shell, etc. has been removed). Toss enough mayonnaise into the crabmeat to loosely bind. Gently fold in the capers. Add salt and freshly ground pepper to taste. Serve with endive or as a filling for cherry tomatoes.

Makes ten servings.

Christopher Blake's Return-to-Normalcy Shrimp Mousse

Bland adapted this recipe from a favorite of the late Christopher Blake, New Orleans bon vivant, restaurateur, and playwright. Whenever Christopher visited Bland's family in Arkansas, he did so by cover of night. Legal reasons, he always said. We felt it best not to press him. He wasn't just the man who came to dinner but the man who cooked dinner, and we wanted him to keep visiting. Christopher, by the way, wrote a play called *The Fair Fair Ladies of Chartres Street*. We hope that they were nice ladies, too, like Belle Watling, the paragon of their profession in *Gone with the Wind*.

This is definitely a nice lady recipe—as long as you wait a decent interval after the interment.

Ingredients

2 cups plain yogurt
1 pound cream cheese, softened
1 cup homemade mayonnaise
6 cups boiled chopped shrimp
2 tablespoons Knox unflavored gelatin
juice of 2 lemons mixed with ¼ cup cold water
½ cup finely minced green onion
½ cup finely minced celery
½ cup finely minced red bell pepper

¼ cup minced pimientos
½ cup salsa picante
½ teaspoon Tabasco
1 teaspoon salt
1 tablespoon Worcestershire sauce (Lea & Perrins)

Mix together the yogurt, cream cheese, and mayonnaise. Fold in the shrimp. Dissolve the gelatin in the lemon juice and cold water, and heat in the top of a double boiler for 5 minutes, stirring.

Fold the gelatin mixture into the cheese/shrimp mixture. Gently add the minced vegetables and seasonings, blending well. Adjust the seasonings. Pour into a 2-quart mold and refrigerate overnight before serving.

Serves twelve.

Smoked Salmon and Horseradish Cream

Smoked salmon and horseradish cream served with tiny onion sandwiches are the quintessence of a nice-lady recipe. We might add that, with a fork, this is also a good first course for company dinner.

Ingredients
    2 teaspoons Knox unflavored gelatin
    6 tablespoons cold water
    ½ cup heavy cream
    2 tablespoons prepared horseradish,
        drained
    2 teaspoons lemon juice
    ¼ teaspoon sugar
    ¾ pound thinly sliced smoked salmon

Sprinkle gelatin over the cold water in a small saucepan. Place pan over low heat and stir until the gelatin is completely dissolved. Allow to cool slightly and then refrigerate for 10 minutes.

Whip the cream until firm and then fold in the horseradish, lemon juice, sugar, and the gelatin mixture. Continue to beat until very thick. Chill.

Place a generous spoonful of the cream mixture down the center of each salmon piece. Gently fold the two sides over so that they overlap slightly. Place each cream-filled salmon roll seam-side down on a baking sheet lined with wax paper. Cover with plastic wrap and chill.

Serve chilled salmon with lightly buttered triangles of pumpernickel bread and lemon wedges, or on a tray with onion sandwiches (recipe follows).

Serves six to eight.

Onion Sandwiches

48 thin bread slices
3 or 4 red onions
salt
$\frac{1}{2}$ cup unsalted butter, softened
1 cup homemade mayonnaise
2 cups finely minced fresh parsley

With a cookie cutter, cut a 2-inch round from each bread slice. Using a very sharp knife, slice the onions into paper-thin rounds. Peel off outer rings to make the onion slices the same size as bread. Salt them lightly.

Lightly butter the bread rounds, and make a sandwich of 2 rounds of bread with an onion slice between. Spread the edges with mayonnaise and roll the sandwiches in minced parsley.

Cover sandwiches and chill at least 1 hour before serving.

Makes two dozen servings.

V. D. Spinach (Visiting Dignitary Spinach)

V. D. Spinach is one of those dishes that has traveled the circuit. It arrived as a vegetable dish for company and somehow has morphed into a stuffing for tiny cocktail tomatoes, and even as a dip for a restorative cocktail party. We are beginning to refer to this as the renaissance dish, because it can do anything.

Ingredients

2 (10-ounce) packages frozen
   chopped spinach
1 (8-ounce) package cream cheese
½ cup melted butter
1 teaspoon lemon juice
1 (14-ounce) can artichokes,
   drained
1 sleeve Ritz crackers
butter

Preheat the oven to 350°.

Cook the spinach according to package directions. Drain well. Add the cream cheese and butter, then the lemon juice. Mix well. Spread in a 9 x 13-inch casserole dish. Quarter the artichokes and place them on top of the spinach.

Roll the Ritz crackers with a rolling pin until they are fine crumbs. Sprinkle the crumbs over the casserole and dot with additional butter.

Bake for 30 minutes, until hot throughout.

Serves ten.

Cheese Biscuits

As we noted earlier, cheese straws, though arguably festive, are served at St. James' funeral receptions. Otherwise, they'd be ideal for the restorative cocktail. To serve something similar that doesn't evoke memories of the funeral, we offer Cheese Biscuits. Be sure to make your biscuits thin. No one from the South likes to serve big anything. It's just not the nice-lady way of doing things.

Ingredients

    2 cups all-purpose flour
    fresh pepper
    lots of cayenne pepper
    2 teaspoons salt
    1 teaspoon dry mustard (preferably Colman's)
    1 cup margarine (Do not substitute butter)
    2+ cups grated extra-sharp cheese
    Tabasco
    4 tablespoons sesame seeds

Combine all of the dry ingredients. Add the margarine and cheese, blending by hand or with a food processor. Add Tabasco and start tasting, correcting the seasoning as needed. Add sesame seeds and incorporate well. You want them evenly distributed throughout the dough.

Do not overwork the dough, as this makes for a tough end product. Form dough into rolls . . . *thin* rolls. Wrap in clear plastic wrap and then foil, and freeze.

When you get ready to cook, slightly thaw the rolls so that they can be sliced easily but retain their shape. Slice about ¼ inch thick.

Preheat the oven to 375°.

Bake slices on ungreased cookie sheets for approximately 10 to 12 minutes, or until slightly brown around the edges and firm to the touch. Cool for a minute or two and remove from the sheets. Be careful not to overcook.

Makes eight dozen.

Faux Dieter's Antipasto

You always want to put out something that satisfies the aesthetic longing for something green. This also gives the impression of being appropriate for dieters, and though utterly delicious and pretty on a table—well, it *looks* dietetic.

Ingredients

2 green peppers, cut in strips
2 red peppers, cut in strips
2 yellow peppers, cut in strips
2 heads cauliflower, separated
    into flowerets
1 bunch celery, cut into sticks
2 bunches carrots, cut into sticks
1 pound of fresh mushrooms (button
    type prefered)
1 ½ cups olive and vegetable oils, mixed
3 cups tarragon vinegar
½ cup sugar
3 cloves garlic, minced
1 tablespoon prepared mustard
1 tablespoon salt
3 teaspoons tarragon leaves
freshly ground pepper

Assemble the prepared vegetables in a very large glass jar with a cover. Combine the remaining ingredients and pour over the vegetables. Marinate overnight, turning the jar occasionally. Drain well before serving. This makes a lot, but it will keep for several weeks in the refrigerator.

Makes at least two dozen servings.

Pickled Mushrooms

In a small town, you don't have to worry about whether they're shitake or portabello. We can only get button mushrooms, and that's what this recipe requires. If you get into talking about old times, these are perfect, and easy to make, and the mushrooms are not likely to be the only things to be pickled.

Ingredients

    4 pounds of cleaned, fresh mushrooms
    1 large onion, chopped
    ½ cup parsley, chopped
    2 cloves garlic, minced
    3 bay leaves
    1 teaspoon dried tarragon
    1 cup white vinegar
    ½ cup olive oil
    2 tablespoons lemon juice
    2 cups white wine
    salt
    freshly ground pepper

In a large saucepan, combine all the above ingredients and bring to a boil. Reduce the heat and continue to cook for approximately 10 minutes. Stir frequently. When mushrooms are tender, remove from the heat at once and refrigerate.

Makes about twelve servings.

Reincarnation Shrimp Dip

People come and people go, but certain recipes will always be around. This is one of them—it keeps reappearing. Maybe it's because it's such a safe bet—it can be made straight from the pantry. No fresh stuff here! But it's delicious, and there's hardly a house in Greenville that doesn't have the ingredients on hand (see The Eternal Pantry, page 64).

Ingredients
2 (6-ounce) cans shrimp
1 (8-ounce) package cream cheese, softened
1 cup sour cream
1/2 cup finely minced green onion
1/2 cup minced celery
juice of 1 or 2 lemons, to taste
salt
freshly ground pepper
red pepper flakes

Drain shrimp and mash.

Mix the cream cheese with sour cream until blended. Add the onions, celery, lemon juice, salt, ground pepper, and red pepper flakes to the mixture. Fold in shrimp and taste for seasoning. Refrigerate until ready to serve. Better the next day!

Makes about one quart.

Curry Dip for Fresh Vegetables

This is another one of those things we're almost embarrassed to admit we love. It's the pineapple casserole of cocktail foods, a dish that blends ketchup and curry power and has only one redeeming feature: People love it. Because it's such a frequent dish, it's almost as closely associated with the restorative cocktail as aspic is with the funeral reception.

Ingredients
    1 cup homemade mayonnaise
    1 ½ tablespoons curry powder
    3 tablespoons ketchup
    1 tablespoon Worcestershire (Lea & Perrins)
    1 teaspoon Tabasco
    2 teaspoons grated onion
    salt to taste

In a jar or other container, mix all the ingredients, cover, and chill for several hours or days. The longer this sits, the better it tastes.

Serves ten.

St. James' Cheese

This is just a mound of cheese. It's something for the den or library.

Ingredients

3 cups finely grated extra-sharp cheddar cheese
2 or 3 tablespoons homemade mayonnaise . . . only
    enough to bind
4 green onions, finely chopped
$^2/_3$ cup chopped pecans
homemade pepper jelly

Combine cheese, mayonnaise, onions, and pecans. Mold on the serving platter and spread hot pepper jelly over the top. Refrigerate.

Bring to room temperature before serving.

Serves twelve.

Hot Pepper Jelly

Ingredients

  ³/₄ cup sweet red or green bell peppers
  ¹/₄ cup hot peppers (about three pods)
  6 ¹/₄ cups sugar
  1 ¹/₄ cups apple cider vinegar
  ¹/₄ cup juice from peppers
  1 bottle Certo

Remove seeds from the peppers. In the bowl of a food processor, coarsely chop peppers (separately). Reserve juice from each.

Bring peppers, sugar, vinegar, and pepper juice to a boil. Keep a rolling boil for six minutes.

Remove from heat and add Certo. Boil one minute. Stir to mix. Skim off foam. Cool for a few minutes. Rinse glass jars with hot water, dry, and add jelly. Seal jars.

Makes six to eight jars.

NOTE: *The really green pepper jelly has a few drops of food coloring added. If you choose, add the coloring to the vinegar.*

Goat Cheese Torta

Ladies in the Delta have always been able to get things they need—a trip to New Orleans with an ice chest or a drive to one of the bigger grocery stores in Memphis always enhances the Delta pantry. We could not get goat cheese fifteen years ago. We could get wonderful things, of course—fresh quail and duck and vegetables that were garden fresh in reality and not just a menu writer's dream. A truck even came up from New Orleans with fresh oysters, and the best oyster loaf in the world was to be had at Frank's Café. But we didn't have goat cheese. Now it's available in our supermarkets.

Ingredients
16 ounces cream cheese, softened
7 to 8 ounces mild goat cheese
2 cloves garlic, minced
4 tablespoons snipped fresh oregano
    or 1 ¼ teaspoons dried, crushed
¼ teaspoon fresh ground pepper
¼ cup prepared pesto
½ cup sun-dried tomatoes packed in oil
2 tablespoons slivered almonds, toasted
fresh oregano for garnish
thinly sliced French bread

Line a 1-quart loaf or soufflé pan with clear plastic wrap. In a food processor, combine cream cheese, goat cheese, garlic, oregano, and pepper. Process until smooth. Spread a third of the cheese mixture in the bottom of the pan. Top with pesto, spreading evenly. Layer with another third of the cheese mixture.

Drain sun-dried tomatoes and chop.

Spread these evenly over the cheese mixture. Cover the sun-dried tomatoes with the remaining cheese. Cover with plastic wrap and press gently to pack it. Chill several hours or overnight.

Remove the plastic wrap. Invert the container and turn the contents onto a serving plate. Garnish torta with toasted almonds and fresh oregano.

Makes twelve servings.

Hot Feta Artichoke Dip

We've been quick to embrace feta cheese—another one of those things we couldn't get until fairly recently in the Deep South—and include it in our repertoire. This is now one of the most popular cocktail accompaniments in the Delta.

Ingredients

1 (14-ounce) can artichokes, drained
1 (4-ounce) package feta cheese, crumbled
1 cup mayonnaise
½ cup shredded Parmesan cheese
2 tablespoons lemon juice
1 teaspoon white pepper
¼ to ½ cup sliced green onions
½ cup chopped tomatoes

Preheat the oven to 350°.

Cut the artichokes into quarters or halves and mix with feta cheese, mayonnaise, Parmesan cheese, lemon juice, and white pepper. Bake in an au gratin dish or shallow 3-cup dish for 20 to 25 minutes, or until browned.

Garnish with sliced green onions and/or chopped tomatoes. Serve with toasted pita triangles or baguette slices.

Makes two cups.

Marinated Ripe Olives

It's a nice idea to keep marinated olives in the refrigerator at all times. This is the sort of thing that goes well with an afternoon gathering, even when there have been no recent reductions in the Delta population (rare as such times are).

Ingredients

    2 large (6-ounce-weight) cans pitted ripe olives,
        drained
    1 large (15-ounce) bottle Worcestershire sauce
        (Lea & Perrins)

Place the well-drained olives in a container and cover with Worcestershire sauce. Cover the container and marinate for several days in the refrigerator. When ready to serve, drain well. These keep for a long time if covered tightly and refrigerated.

Makes 3 cups.

Salted Pecans

We like to pick up the pecans out of our own yards, but it is perfectly all right to use store-bought pecans. What's not perfectly all right is to think we say PEE-cans. This is an ugly canard spread by the same people who put it out that we say PRAY-leens. We say pecans and pralines, almost, though not exactly, like you say them.

1 tablespoon butter
1 teaspoon Tabasco
⅓ cup Worcestershire sauce (Lea & Perrins)
1 teaspoon salt
2 cups pecan halves

Preheat the oven to 300°.

Melt the butter in a skillet over low heat. Remove from heat and add the Tabasco, Worcestershire, and salt. Stir in pecans and mix well. Each piece should be well coated. Spread pecans on a baking sheet and toast for approximately 15 minutes. Stir once or twice during cooking. Drain on paper towels.

Makes two cups.

Index